ב"ה

Full
throttle
Spring Greetings
Tom

think you & the
audience will enjoy
this
best wishes
barry

The JOY of Living:

How to Slay Stress and Be Happy

by Barry Shore

Published by

Joy of Living Institute Publishing

811 Appleby St

Venice, CA 90291

Cover Photo By: Jonah Light

The Joy of Living

Barry Shore

ISBN 978-1-930376-15-1

Printed in the United States of America

First Printing, 2021
Second Printing, 2021

To my wife, Naomi,

without whom I would just be protoplasm

Table of Contents

Foreword

Imagine...You walk out of Your office to meet someone and there stands... Moses!

And he hands You a KEEP SMILING Card.

Yes. Thar's what it was like when I met Barry Shore, The Ambassador of JOY, on an August day for our interview.

Replete with white beard, flowing hair, a radiant smile, and a 7 foot tall magical wand. That's how it felt. Magical. You see Barry is an energetic being (combination of Richard Simmons and Tony Robbins I say) whose soul/sole focus is to bring JOY into the world. He does this with a special joie de vivre and this book is the embodiment of that spirit.

You'll learn much. And as we discussed in our interview, JOY is that special quality that makes one Healthier, Wealthier and Wiser.

And who doesn't want that!

This is a good book by a good guy.

Wishing you all more JOY in your life!

PS: And then, just before the interview began, he paused and broke out Singing his own unique version of a Happy Birthday Song (it was my birthday just days before). Truly one of the Best Interviews I've ever had. En-JOY!

— **Jack Canfield**, Coauthor of the #1 New York Times bestselling *Chicken Soup for the Soul*® series and *The Success Principles*™: *How to Get from Where You Are to Where You Want to Be*

Preface

"Mr. Shore, can You hear me? Mr. Shore, if You can hear me, please blink."

It was a soft voice—feminine, yet commanding.

My eyes blinked.

"Good," the voice responded. "My name is Dr. Abrekov. I'm the neurologist on staff for the weekend. Mr. Shore, You have something very serious. It could be fatal. I need to run some tests. Are You with me? Please blink twice if You understand me."

My eyes blinked. Twice.

Serious? That meant it could be something fatal. Nothing was moving except my eyes. I tried turning my head. It moved ever so slightly. I was in a room, apparently. Not heaven. Or another place. I was in a place with people.

Now I was recalling some of the events of the past twelve hours. Getting up from a nap. Falling down. Getting up. Dressing. Walking to the front of the house. Sitting in my chair. And...not moving. Calling out for my son, Ezra. Asking him to please get Dr. Karz. Dr. Karz came over. He looked at me and called his brother—also Dr. Karz—my primary care physician. "Get him to the hospital. I'll meet him there."

Soon it was clear that I was paralyzed. Completely paralyzed. Within a matter of hours, my entire body shut down. No car accident. No spinal injury. A rare disease attacked my peripheral nervous system and shut me down.

Life as I knew it was over.

STRESS entered my life on September 17, 2004. I capitalize the word because this is the level of STRESS that tests Your very being. This short book that You are reading is a tribute (strange word?) to the STRESS I encountered—STRESS that I then countered with JOY.

It was and is a struggle. However, the result of that struggle was so life changing that it must be discussed and shared.

And so, I am. With You.

In the ensuing years I've managed, with the help of family, friends, and God, to formulate and now articulate 11 Strategies that enable me to live in JOY, under all circumstances and vicissitudes. I gladly share these with You in the knowledge that You will benefit from learning about them and utilizing those that resonate with You.

The journey is just that: a journey. We all encounter issues, but that doesn't have to be the end of our stories. May we be able to help one another and learn to lift each other up through the pouring forth of what I feel is the greatest healer of all: JOY.

Most sincere best wishes for Your continuing success,

barry

P.S. You'll be encountering wordplay throughout this book. Some will make You SMILE, some may make You groan. Feel free to add Your own and let me hear what You discover.

Testimonials

Take it from the WishMan, The JOY of LIVING will help You.

Frank Shankwitz, The Creator and Co-Founder of The Make-A-Wish Foundation.

When Beach Money was first published in 2008 it spoke to people's potential to earn and to dream. I know people also yearn to live happier and more fulfilling lives. My friend Barry Shore fills that need with The JOY of LIVING. Pick it up. Use it. You'll FEEL the JOY!

Jordan Adler, Network Marketer Extraordinaire, Author and "Dream Broker"

Our friend and mentor Barry Shore is truly a Next Gen-er. He's 72 chronologically; 46 metabolically (swims 2miles/day!); mental acuity is 28 (he hangs around us); and his SOW is 8. We highly recommend you read his latest book, The JOY of LIVING, to learn about SOW. The book serves as a road-map to help you slay stress and be happy, as Barry inspires all in the Next Generation to be healthier and wealthier.

Dylan and Justin, Founders of Next Gen HQ

Barry shore is a game changer... this is his playbook. No doubt this book will change your life forever... it will enlighten, encourage, inspire, uplift, motivate exhilarate, elucidate and bring out the innermost smile of your soul.

Rabbi Z Novoseller, Executive Director, EPI Networking

Barry is true inspiration. His spirit shines bright and brings hope to those around him. As an Ambassador of Joy, Barry's testimony of going from tragedy to triumph lights a path we can all follow.

Steve Gatena, founder of pray.com

If you want to experience JOY, I recommend you get a copy for yourself and for all the people you want to share JOY with!

Ken "Dr. Smiley" Rochon, Jr., PhD. Co-Founder: The Keep Smiling Movement

Barry Shore on the page is almost as ebullient as he is in person. This book is full of infectious energy and well-argued reasons to make the most of every precious moment.

Michael Medved, national talk show host, film critic, author of 14 books, and frequent columnist for major newspapers including the New York Times, Wall Street Journal, USA Today

Wonderful wisdom from a whacky, worldly, wondrous Illuminator. Barry always shares ideas and inspiration like only few can. Read this book thoroughly and you'll benefit. I did- you will too.

David M. Corbin, Two time WSJ Best Selling Author

I often wonder what the world would be like with more people like Barry Shore. His positive attitude is infectious. Barry brings light to even the darkest room. You'd think his electric positivity is impossible to maintain until you're fortunate enough to call him a friend of over twenty years, as I have. We should all consider ourselves lucky for the opportunity to listen to what Barry Shore has to say.

Stone Melet, Successful serial Entrepreneur. Founder of BestofLegacy.com

The Joy Of Living is written by the best JOYologist on the planet! Barry Shore turned tragedy into triumph and his infectious smile and heartfelt singing instantly places you in the most beautiful of trances. Even Oprah selected Barry's philanthropic platform as one of her favorite things! Now Barry has shared his extraordinary formula for creating JOY in any situation with you in this elegant masterpiece, The Joy Of Living! Read this book and start living a more joyful life today!

Tim Shurr, MA, author of One Belief Away! And organizer of Legends Summit

Barry Shore's new book "The JOY of Living: How to Slay Stress and Be Happy" is full of insights and lessons that can help you incorporate more Happiness and Joy into your life. You will learn how to choose happiness and see miracles in life every day. Barry not only teaches you how to incorporate Joy into your life, but he shows you how it is done. I recommend that you buy his book today.

David Riklan, Founder of SelfGrowth.com

Barry is one of the few people on this planet that truly lives every day focused on joy and sharing it with others. If you could learn from someone, this is your guy. Expect Great Things.

Greg Jacobson, Happiness Strategist HappilyAchieving.org

Barry is the life source of calm reality to millions! Read and practice his strategies and You will Live Well!

Laurie McDermott, TheWifeExpert.com

How I Turned Tragedy into Joy

I am the man who went from happy, healthy, and whole to being paralyzed—overnight.

And it wasn't due to a sudden-but-obvious tragedy, like an automobile accident or a spinal injury. Instead, it was caused by a rare neurological disease—not the sort of thing You can just "bounce back" from.

In fact, it was the sort of thing some people don't come back from at all.

But I did come back from it and, as I started to regain my physical abilities, I built a system that enables people everywhere to live in JOY daily—no matter the circumstances. I took what I learned in my whole life journey—from my business successes and failures, from my severe health challenges, and from my addiction to medication—to articulate the 3 Fundamentals of Life.

Those Fundamentals changed me, and they can change You too.

Meet the Ambassador of JOY. My Mission is to transform the whole world through JOY. And thankfully, the message is indeed being embraced globally.

I resolved to use the 3 Fundamentals of Life to live in JOY, daily.

The Fundamentals are:

1. Life has a Purpose.
2. Living with Purpose enables You to GO MAD: Go Make a Difference.
3. You can unlock the power and secrets of everyday words and terms to see miracles.

Together, we'll use these principles to explore Your life. By the end of this book, You will be able to utilize these principles Yourself. They will enable You to live a healthier, wealthier, wiser life.

I'll also share the stories of the people who helped me learn these valuable insights. Their stories will illuminate Your story, and so I can't wait for You to meet them.

Elijah. Terrible T. Mr. Marsh. Mr. Campbell. Aida. Susan. Francis.

Above all, Frances.

And even above Frances, Naomi.

Together, we'll learn the lessons they taught and see how simple acts, words, and thoughts can and do Make A Difference.

I can teach these lessons because I learned them myself, and I learned them the hard way. I was many months in hospital and rehab units; two years in a hospital bed in my own home, unable to turn over by myself; four years in wheelchairs; eighteen months with braces on both legs from my hips to my ankles—and believe me, even if it sounds awful, getting that metal exoskeleton was progress.

Today I am able to be vertical and ambulatory with the help of a six-and-a-half-foot walking wand made for me by a Zen master. But I still can't walk up a stair—or even a curb—by myself, and I have help twelve hours per day, seven days per week. However, I remain positive, purposeful, powerful, and pleasant.

And all because of the 11 Strategies for Living in JOY, daily.

Oh, and I learned to swim.

I use flotation devices on both my legs to keep from sinking, paddles on my hands because my fingers don't close, and a snorkel for breathing.

But it's still me, swimming, when I used to not even be able to roll over in my bed.

Now I'm able to swim two miles per day. Six days per week.

And, as of publication date, I have accumulated 7,891 miles. Yes, it's a lot.

Imagine going from being quadriplegic to swimming the distance from Venice Beach, California (my hometown) to Hawaii, then down to Fiji, and way down under to Sydney, Australia.

The way I envisioned JOY enabled me to swim, to smile, and, as I did so, to keep miling (pun fully intended).

My own recovery led me to a new vision for my life. I saw that God had invited me to deepen my commitment to helping others and to learning more about myself. I could take my success in business and teach others how to have abundance. I could take my journey toward health and help others do the same. I saw that my enthusiasm for life could help move people to an inner celebration of the eternal in each moment.

I am so grateful that my journey is bringing such joy to people.

The seeming disaster has opened a call to adventure and a journey that revealed my deep connection to family, friends, and all living beings. It has cemented the certainty that JOY does heal. It has demonstrated that anyone can choose joy to heal the stresses in life.

I looked at every facet of my life for inspiration. I know that You have the same capacity, and that You are a golden ray of sunshine with a brilliant soul, and that Your being can light up the universe. I am certain of that.

I've been where You are. I've experienced deep pain: physical, mental and spiritual. I've experienced untold STRESS: physical, mental, and spiritual. Business successes and failure; making millions, losing millions, and bankruptcy. I've known addiction and near-death experiences—twice.

I've been where You are…and You can be where I am. Living in JOY, daily.

In picking up this book, You are investing a little bit of money, Your energy, and Your most valuable possession: Your time. Take this adventure with me to the most exuberant point of Your life.

Welcome.

Let's create a JOY that will energize the world.

Let's go Make A Difference!

PART 1

The Problem: What Kills Us? Stress

Not directly. More like death by a thousand sighs.

It's insidious. Invidious, invasive, and, if continuous and not stopped, will ruin Your physical, mental, and spiritual being.

Stress is a common occurrence. While You can't remove every stressor from Your life, it's possible to manage and reduce stress and maintain Your health. This is important because chronic stress can cause mental fatigue, irritability, sleeplessness, obesity, skin ailments, heart issues, anxiety, depression, and gastrointestinal problems.

Yes, that list of symptoms observed across the population tells You that You're not alone in this battle.

But even when You know the physical and mental effects of stress, You may be unaware of the different stages of stress, known as general adaptation syndrome (GAS). When You understand the different stages of stress and how the body responds in these stages, it's easier to identify signs of chronic stress in Yourself.

I'm writing this in the year 2020. The world is beset with panic, disease, and economic and societal ruin.

Right now, the most searched word in the world after Covid (and its related causes/cures) is STRESS. It's affecting everyone.

STRESS is an acronym that I use to describe how to deal with the effects of untoward circumstances. Essentially there are three factors that cause STRESS.

These are and have always been:

- Money
- Work
- Home

Yes, these are universal and constant. Even in the best of times.

There are however two divergent ways to deal with STRESS, both revealed in my insights.

STRESS can stand for: Stomach-Turning Reality… Enabling Self-Sabotage.

There is little need to go into depth regarding each of the three stressors above. It is self-evident that money issues can and do cause tremendous pressures. The same for work. And, certainly, for home/family. Often in times of recession and disaster, these factors are intertwined and exacerbate one another. They truly cause a stomach-turning reality.

STRESS can also mean: Stomach-Turning Reality…Enabling Self-Success.

Same exact situation/s dealt with in a different way/s. Your response to the stomach-turning reality makes all the difference. Struggling is the continual and real test of life. And it's something we all face every single day.

How You deal with the reality of these issues determines how Your physical and mental wellbeing will be affected. Certainly, You can't be cavalier. Yet You can utilize practices, tips, and tools to enable You to direct Your mind and guide Your body to avoid falling prey to a pity party which can lead to the use/abuse of medications, alcohol, or to other aberrant behavior.

Mind is the master. Once You grasp this fundamental fact and leverage this powerful tool, You can and will achieve success under all circumstances and vicissitudes.

How do You maintain inner strength during stressful periods?

Consider a submarine. As the ship goes down, the pressure (strength) inside needs to increase to counterbalance the pressure outside. Likewise, when we are in stressful situations, we must make sure our internal strength is adequate to offset the external forces pushing against us.

Anger also produces stress. Have You ever known people whose lives seemed to have a thin veneer of civility and calm, yet once the surface was scratched, anger bubbled up like a volcano? Stress and anger go hand-in-glove.

We also know that there are two types of stress: vertical and horizontal. The vertical is healthy because it pulls You up. Think of a flower on a stem. Without turgor pressure, the stem droops. Without the fluids pushing through the cells, the flower dies. We can grow limp as well. A useful example of the sort of pressure that pulls us up is the sense of awe or reverence of God.

Horizontal stresses pull us apart and create damage. Designing our lives to meet others' demands and standards is horizontal. All the current talk about self-image leads to horizontal stress. I do not mean that we should have no concept of self-worth. But we want to have a clear definition of self-worth that comes from knowing we were brought into this world for a purpose. That knowledge is a settled knowledge and doesn't change just because of what others think or say.

In our competitive society there is another prevailing stress—the fear of losing. The specter of losing by our choosing stresses us. When we make one decision, we give up other options. These are the "Y" points. Marriage and career are two of the biggest examples. One of the pitfalls of our current day is buyer's remorse. "If I choose the left fork and it grows dull, I opt out and choose another road." This is a mistake. The stress of always looking around for the better option steals the joy of commitment.

The true test of life is never in what happens to us.

It is always in how we choose to respond to situations.

As we'll learn later in the 11 Strategies, the six most important words You can learn and internalize are:

Choice, not chance, determines Your destiny.

Repeat this. Often. Think about it. Internalize and utilize.

Choice, not chance, determines Your destiny.

What Is the General Adaptation Syndrome Relating to STRESS?

GAS is the three-stage process that describes the physiological changes the body goes through when under stress. Hans Selye, a medical doctor and researcher, came up with the theory of GAS. During an experiment at McGill University in Montreal, he observed a series of physiological changes in rats after they were exposed to stressful events.

With additional research, Selye concluded that these changes were not an isolated case, but rather the typical response to stress. Selye identified these three stages as: Alarm, Resistance, and Exhaustion. Understanding these different responses and how they relate to each other may help You cope with stress.

Alarm Reaction Stage

The alarm reaction stage refers to the initial symptoms the body experiences when under stress. You may be familiar with the "fight-or-flight" response, which is a physiological response to stress. This natural reaction prepares You to either flee or protect Yourself in dangerous situations. Your heart rate increases, Your adrenal gland releases cortisol (a stress hormone), and You receive a boost of adrenaline, which increases energy. This fight-or-flight response occurs in the alarm reaction stage.

Resistance Stage

After the initial shock of a stressful event and having a fight-or-flight response, the body begins to repair itself. It releases a lower amount of cortisol, and Your heart rate and blood pressure begin to normalize. Although Your body enters this recovery phase, it retains vestiges of its high-alert stage for a while. If You overcome stress and the situation is no longer an issue, Your body continues to repair itself until Your hormone levels, heart rate, and blood pressure reach a pre-stress state.

Now, here's the nub of the issue: The term "allostasis" has been coined to clarify ambiguities associated with the word "stress." Allostasis refers to the adaptive processes that maintain homeostasis through the production of mediators such as adrenalin, cortisol and other chemical messengers. These mediators of the stress response promote adaptation in the aftermath of acute stress, but they also contribute to allostatic overload, the wear and tear on the body and brain that result from being "stressed out." This conceptual framework has created a need to know how to improve the efficiency of the adaptive response to stressors while minimizing overactivity of the same systems, since such overactivity results in many of the common diseases of modern life. This framework has also helped to demystify the biology of stress by emphasizing the protective as well as the damaging effects of the body's attempts to cope with the challenges known as stressors.[1] This chronic stress begins to harm the mind and body if left unresolved.

Your body continues to secrete the stress hormone cortisol. You may think You're managing stress well, but Your body's physical response tells a different story. If the resistance stage continues for too long of a period without pauses to offset the effects of stress, this can lead to the exhaustion stage.

Exhaustion Stage

This is the result of ineffective coping with stress or an environment that keeps on stressing us out. You are on stress overload and the wear and tear on the body and brain cause or make worse most problems in life. Struggling with stress for long periods can drain Your physical, emotional, and mental resources to the point where Your body no longer has strength to fight stress.

Signs of exhaustion include chronic diseases, compromised immune system functioning and mental health problems, including:

- fatigue
- high blood pressure
- sleeplessness
- burnout
- infectious diseases
- heart disease
- depression
- gastrointestinal problems
- diabetes
- anxiety
- obesity
- addiction

---

1   https://www.ncbi.nlm.nih.gov/pmc/articles/PMC1197275/

You may give up or feel Your situation is hopeless. A feeling of hopelessness is a dangerous place to be. The good news is the 11 Strategies will give You the ability to increase hope.

The physical effects of this stage also weaken Your immune system and put You at risk for stress-related illnesses.

When Does General Adaptation Syndrome Occur?

GAS can occur with any type of stress. Stressful events can include:

- a job loss, or even promotion
- medical problems
- financial troubles
- family breakdown
- trauma

And now for the good news: while stress is unpleasant, the upside is that knowledge of these stages can actually improve how Your body responds to stressors, particularly in the alarm stage.

The fight-or-flight response that occurs in the alarm stage is for Your protection. A higher hormone level during this stage benefits You. It gives You more energy and improves Your concentration, so You can focus and tackle the situation. When stress is short-term or short-lived, the alarm stage isn't harmful.

You must learn to think and say that STRESS can be a positive situation—note the acronym here. STRESS, when handled well, stands for: Stomach-Turning Reality (yes, admitting to the facts is vital!) Enabling (yes, this will actually benefit me!) Self-Success (truly!).

Numerous studies over the past three decades have shown that over 86% of people in situations which they considered the "ruinous, terrible, awful, worse possible situation" found that it turned out to be "beneficial, cloud with silver lining, best possible situation, amazing results."

What? 86%! How can that be? Because mind is the master. When You allow and enable Your mind to review, let go, and dispense with blame and complaints, You are empowering Your essence to serve. (We'll talk more about this in the Strategy about Don't Complain, Don't Blame.)

This isn't the case with prolonged/chronic stress. The longer You leave stress unresolved, the more harmful it is to Your health. You also don't want to remain in the resistance stage for too long and risk entering the exhaustion stage. Once You're in the exhaustion stage, prolonged stress raises the risk for chronic high blood pressure, stroke, heart disease, and depression. You also have a higher risk for infections and cancer due to a weaker immune system.

The Effects of Stress on Your Body

You're sitting in traffic, late for an important meeting, watching the minutes tick away. Your hypothalamus, a tiny control tower in Your brain, decides to send out the order: send in the stress hormones! These stress hormones are the same ones that trigger Your body's "fight or flight" response. Your heart races, Your breath quickens, and Your muscles tense for action. This response was designed to protect Your body in an emergency by preparing You to react quickly. But when the stress response keeps firing, day after day, it can put Your health at serious risk.

With the 11 Strategies for Living in JOY, daily, we will learn practical tips and tools to reduce, mitigate, and even eliminate most stressors. You will be living a healthier and thereby wealthier, and wiser life. Let's move forward.

EFFECTS OF STRESS ON YOUR BODY

headaches
Stress can trigger and
intensify tension headaches.

heartburn
Stress increases the production of
stomach acid, which could lead to
heartburn or make it worse.

rapid breathing
When you're stressed, the
muscles that help you breathe
tense up, which can leave you
short of breath.

risk of heart attack
Over time, an increased heart rate
and high blood pressure damage
your arteries, which could lead to a
heart attack.

pounding heart
Stress hormones make your
heart pump faster so that blood
can quickly reach your vital
organs and limbs.

fertility problems
Stress interferes with the
reproductive system in both
men and women, and may
make it harder to conceive.

erectile dysfunction
Your brain plays an important part in
the process of getting an erection.
Stress can interfere with this process.

Missed Periods
Fluctuating hormones can throw your
menstrual cycle off, or in severe cases
stop it altogether.

increased depression
Chronic stress can wear you down
emotionally and lead to depression.

insomnia
Stress makes it harder to fall
asleep and stay asleep, which
can lead to insomnia.

weakened immune system
Long-term stress weakens your
immune system's defenses, leaving
you more vulnerable to infections.

high blood sugar
release extra sugar (glucose)
into your bloodstream, which
over time puts you at risk for
type 2 diabetes.

high blood pressure
Stress hormones tighten
blood vessels, which can
raise your blood pressure.

stomachache
Stress affects your body's
digestive system, which can
lead to stomachaches, nausea,
and other tummy troubles.

low sex drive
Stress - and the fatigue that
often comes with it - can
take a toll on your libido.

tense muscles
Stress makes muscles tense
up, and chronic stress can lead
to tension-related headaches
and backaches.

The Takeaways

There are two alternative definitions of STRESS.

Since it's not possible to eliminate every stressor, it's important to find ways to reduce, mitigate, and cope with stress.

Knowing the signs and stages of stress can help You take appropriate steps to manage Your stress level and lower Your risk of complications.

It's essential for You to train Your mind and body to repair and recover not later than the resistance stage. If not, Your risk for exhaustion rises.

By utilizing the 11 Strategies, You will learn practical practices, tips, and tools to maintain and achieve a JOY-filled life, no matter the circumstances.

The Solution: JOY is our Healer

Essentially, there are three factors that cause JOY.

These are, and have been since time immemorial:

- Money
- Work
- Home (family/friends)

Sound familiar? Yes, they're the same three that cause STRESS.

STRESS works from the outside in. It uses force and pressure to wreak its havoc.

JOY, which is more powerful, works from the inside out. It uses thoughts, words, and deeds to create and build its world.

Later, we will discuss the distinction between excitement and enthusiasm. You'll learn how to moderate the former and increase the latter. This one insight alone will give You renewed hope and vigor.

You will learn to hear the "N" word and smile.

This "N" word is NO. By hearing KNOW every time someone says "no", You will appreciate the insight of understanding that KNOW means:

Knowledge and **W**isdom surround what others render as **negative**. (**K** and **W** around **no**.)

Just as jujitsu uses the opponent's own force against him in ways that force him to submit, so too JOY enables You to gently and decisively defeat the negative forces threatening You and those You love. In more contemporary terms, jujitsu is the gentle art of folding clothes while people are still wearing them. (Aha!)

JOY involves Your thoughts, words, and deeds. Joy expands Your consciousness; calms Your senses. Joy enables You to navigate the most turbulent seas; Joy is the wellspring of LIFE.

LIFE stands for **L**iving **I**nspirationally **F**or **E**ternity.

Yes, when you consciously realize that though Your body is finite, Your spirit is infinite, You gain an additional benefit of living in JOY.

Molding and leveraging Your thoughts, words, and deeds will enable You and all around You to live the life that others call "lucky." Yes, luck can be a most serendipitous occurrence. It usual accompanies, follows, and is attracted to the ones who pursue JOY.

Essentially JOY opens the channels to bring You greater health, wealth, and wisdom. And who doesn't want that?

Think for a moment of some of the most successful people You know, and You will "see" their beaming beings, both internally and externally.

It's a widely accepted belief that living happily and joyfully will vastly improve Your quality of life, and that belief is not unjustified. As we'll see, there's some scientific proof that JOY can do wonders for Your overall health.

Let's look at four ways JOY can have a positive impact on your health.

Let's Start with Your Brain

Your brain is a most marvelous and complex organ made up of multiple lobes and cortexes, all working together to help You function in daily life. Consider the fact that we have more than 400 billion brain cells each with 10,000 neural connections. These, in turn, allow You to have four trillion chemical reactions every second. Yes, thankfully You have 80,000 heart beats per day and 45,000 breaths. All without even a moment's thought on Your part.

And all these neural connections are there for more than deciding what kind of latte you want this morning.

According to Dr. Diana Samuel at Columbia University Medical Center, two parts of your brain specifically work together to produce responses to emotions and emotions in response to stimuli.

The frontal lobe supervises what emotion You are experiencing at any point in time, while the thalamus sends signals to execute Your body's response to the emotion You are feeling.

The hormones serotonin and dopamine are essential in stimulating happiness as a mood, and these two parts of the brain working together trigger the release of these hormones.

When Your brain perceives something that brings You JOY or causes You to smile, the lobes recognize it and, in a sense, wake Your body up in more ways than just emotionally—all as a result of Your choice to respond to something in a positive manner.

All of Your Hormones

The hormones mentioned above, as well as many other hormones contained in the human body (such as oxytocin), all correlate to an emotion or a functioning part of the body.

And then there are endorphins, which are structurally similar to the drug morphine, and are considered natural painkillers because they activate opioid receptors in the brain that help minimize discomfort. They can also help bring about feelings of euphoria and general well-being.

The happy hormones are the ones you want to make more and more of, as much as you can.

Dopamine, oxytocin, serotonin, and endorphins (DOSE) are famously the happy hormones that promote positive feelings like pleasure, joy, and even love.

Dr. Melissa Bonasera has noted that smiling and using those few facial muscles to smile actually causes a release of dopamine and serotonin. And get this: it works even if the smile is fake.

To get Your daily dose of happiness, all You have to do is smile!

Smile, Smile, and Smile Again

You do know it takes twice as many muscles to form a frown as opposed to a smile, don't You?

In a study done by Kansas University, participants were assigned stressful tasks while keeping small sticks in their mouths to force them to stay in a smiling position.

Another test group was told to keep genuine smiles while doing the tasks, and the third control group was told to do the tasks without smiling.

It was proven repeatedly that both the genuine and fake smilers had a lower heart rate and quicker recovery than the non-smilers.

Give your heart a rest and smile whenever You can. Joy is a natural result.

I love smiling so much, I created KEEP SMILING cards and the Keep Smiling Movement that brightens everyone's day.[2] Millions of KEEP SMILING cards have been distributed worldwide. All for *free*. Yes, You can join this worthy endeavor.

---

2 https://www.barryshore.com/smile

Other Organ Systems

Any reaction from Your circulatory system is dependent on Your emotions and JOY is certainly the cause of the more pleasant ones, such as feeling beautiful butterflies in Your stomach or Your face flushing with enthusiasm.

Our body feels good and even better when we experience these feelings from JOY.

When You are joyful, Your breathing comes more easily and smoothly, Your digestion is better, and overall, everything works better inside of You.

And one of the best ways to produce these natural highs is through exercise. Whatever Your preferred physical exercise, You can produce a dose of JOY by being active. What a gift: the ability to move and get happy. My favorite is swimming. Especially when done outdoors in the summer, fall, and spring. (And in southern California, even in the winter!)

The Fountain of Youth

The Fountain of Youth is a mythical spring that restores the youth of anyone who drinks or bathes in its waters. Tales of such a fountain have been recounted around the world for thousands of years.

The myth of these waters reveals the desire of people to discover the elixir that restores vitality.

You have discovered it: JOY. This is an acronym for Jenerating Ongoing Youth.

This production of ongoing youth is the result of learning to live in JOY, daily.

And these are some of the health benefits of living in JOY:

- Longevity
- A regular state of being calm and aware
- Becoming purpose-driven
- Increased brain stimulation
- A more active lifestyle
- The boosting of Your immune system
- Decreased pain
- Stress reduction
- Better sex
- Opening and unclogging of the twin channels of giving and receiving

How to Get More Deep Sleep

Here is the most beneficial restorative process of all: sleep.

Sleep is the miracle cure.

Deep sleep, also referred to as slow-wave sleep (SWS), is one of four stages of sleep (light, deep, REM, and wake) that You spend time in each night. It is known as the "physically restorative" stage of sleep and is of great importance for anyone looking to perform at their best on a daily basis.

I'll briefly explore what You can do to get more deep sleep, including which behaviors I've found help people increase time spent in this highly beneficial sleep stage.

Deep sleep is when Your body restores itself physically. The vast majority of human growth hormone (95%) is actually produced at this time. Something many people don't realize is that You don't actually get stronger at the gym or when You're exercising. Your muscles break down while You're working out, then they are built back up again during deep sleep. Getting enough deep sleep is essential for maximizing potential gains from Your day.

Additionally, deep sleep helps strengthen Your immune system, regenerate cells to repair bone and tissue, stimulate blood flow to muscles, and balance Your metabolism and blood sugar levels.

Any efforts You can make to improve Your overall sleep behavior will tend to benefit Your deep sleep as well. The most basic thing to do is simply spend more time in bed. There are more practical tips and useful suggestions to be found at the website of the National Sleep Foundation.[3]

In general, deep sleep usually consists of 15-25% of most adults' total time asleep. Interestingly enough, when You sleep in your own bed (as opposed to somewhere else), on average You get fifteen additional minutes of total sleep, with three minutes of that (20%) being deep sleep.

---

3   https://www.sleepfoundation.org/articles/healthy-sleep-tips.

Some sleep-promoting behaviors specifically boost deep sleep at a higher-than-expected ratio when compared to overall sleep time:

- **Ear plugs** while sleeping.
- **Breathwork** to relieve stress, either during the day or prior to sleep.
- **Steam room** and **sauna**, with the dry heat of a sauna correlating with a greater proportional increase in deep sleep.
- **More plants in Your diet**. This is obviously a more significant lifestyle choice, but often people average two additional minutes of sleep, with half of that (one minute) being deep sleep.

Here are some (now obvious) deep-sleep inhibitors:

Stress. Feeling stressed causes an average of eight fewer minutes of sleep per night, and one minute less of deep sleep.

Screen device in bed. Use of a screened device in bed corresponds with a one-minute decrease in total sleep and deep sleep.

Shared bed. Although people average twelve more minutes of sleep per night when they share a bed with another person, they actually lose one minute of deep sleep. This doesn't come as a surprise though: noises and movements from Your partner in bed may often diminish Your sleep quality.

And in the "common sense" department, consuming alcohol before bed can be extremely detrimental to deep sleep. When Your body is forced to process alcohol during sleep it has trouble getting beyond light sleep and into deep sleep.

Become a POThead (No, Really!)

Now, let's revisit Your brain.

I have long been a POT advocate, because I learned decades ago that the Power Of Thought is the most potent healing mechanism available. I learned it from my own situations and by studying the processes that were articulated and documented by Norman Cousins (in Anatomy of an Illness) and Dr. Bruce Lipton (in The Biology of Belief: Unleashing the Power of Consciousness, Matter & Miracles).

Norman Cousins essentially self-cured himself of a debilitating and life-threatening disease through a most unusual protocol: laughter! Yes, when You read the story and watch a video or two, You might be incredulous, but it's all true. And not anecdotal.

Dr. Lipton specifically discusses the power of the Three T's:

- Toxins
- Trauma
- Thoughts

It's certainly worth reading his now classic works, but suffice to say that the first two powerful, often life-altering situations of Toxins and Trauma (both of which Your humble author has struggled with) do not even come close to affecting the person/patient as much as Thoughts do. What You think makes all the difference.

(Here's one more helpful word for You to consider: THINK= To Harness Insightful Neural Konnections.)

The Takeaways

Joy heals. It's a natural part of Your being. You have the power to use and leverage Your positive, purposeful, powerful, pleasant essence to live in JOY, daily.

How we see and respond to a "stomach-turning reality" is the key to success or the opposite. Our response to the situation is everything.

By learning, utilizing, and internalizing the 11 Strategies for Living in JOY, daily, You will be able to choose Your course and Your destiny.

Smiling works wonders.

Sleep is the miracle cure.

PART 2

Strategy One: Keep It Simple: S.M.I.L.E

"Bag of peanuts for a dime. Three bags for a quarter. Fifteen cents each in the ballpark."

His voice was raspy as it rang out, but the message was clear: good deal here.

"Hey kid," he said to me, "C'mere. Let me show You how to sell."

Teach me how to sell! Hey, I'm already the best seller of scorecards around. That's how I earned this coveted spot at the corner of Van Ness outside the main grandstand entrance to Fenway Park. I knew what I was doing. Twelve years old and full of piss and vinegar (as we used to say). But hey, this old man sitting on an empty milk crate was certainly doing a brisk business. And he had a captivating smile.

"Yes, sir. What can You teach me?"

"Depends. Let me hear Your method again?"

I called out, "Get Your scorecard here...hey, get Your scorecard here!"

He said, "Good voice. Clear. But where's the benefit? Where's Your why?"

So, I told him, "The scorecards in the park sell for twenty-five cents. Mine are eight cents but everybody gives me a dime." I gotta admit: I thought I was pretty clever, with my unspoken two-cent bump on every sale.

"Okay," he said, "great. So, here's Your new method: *Scorecards here—only eight cents. Twenty-five in the park!*"

Yeah. That made sense... and it turned out to make me a lot of cents. Wow!

I was now doubling my sales and took home $3.25 for ninety minutes of selling...and more often than not, I got to go see the game too. For free. Heaven for a twelve-year-old in Boston in 1960. (By the way, $3.25 in 1960 is the equivalent of $26 in 2020!)

Elijah taught me a lot. Sure, I sold more that season and the next two, but I also learned about life. "See the miracles, kid." That was his refrain. See the miracles.

Elijah was born in Tennessee in 1897. He joined the army and fought in a segregated unit in France in WWI. He asked me, "What do You like to read?" I told him I liked history. He asked what period I liked. Mostly ancient, I responded. Especially Rome. "Do You have any idea of the reality of war?" I told him that of course I did. "No," he said. "No, You don't."

So, he told me he had taken part in many of the fiercest battles of the war. Many soldiers had fallen all about him. I asked him what he was thinking about as the bullets were flying and he was in the trenches.

He replied, "The first time, I said goodbye to the world and asked God to keep my soul. I said it with deep emotion. The second time, I threw myself into the trench and the fear was not as great. By the third and fourth time, even though the casualties were greater, my fear was gone. I looked around and felt certain that I would survive. I learned to see the miracles in life. Everyday."

Powerful. Especially for a twelve-year-old.

And then he said this, "You've heard of Wilma Rudolph?"

"Of course," I said. "She's the fastest woman in the world and won gold in the 1956 and 1960 Olympics! She is *amazing*!"

He said, "She's my first cousin. Did You know that she had polio as a kid? Wore a leg brace until she was twelve. She was raised by her mother and she was the twentieth of twenty-two siblings—and they all helped her with daily massages and encouragement. She was tough. Never gave up and was a spark to everyone. She saw the miracles. Oh, did she see miracles."

That's the lesson for living life successfully: see the miracles. Thank You, Elijah.

SMILE-ing at the Miracles

This strategy is my personal favorite. It resonates with me. For You, this may be the place where You begin the journey. The SMILE. When You understand it's about seeing miracles, then it emanates from Your very being—the heart and the mind. It becomes Your persona.

No longer will Your mood dictate who You are. But Your mind will. Look at the word *mood*. It's really *doom* spelled backwards, and Your mood will become Your doom if You let it dominate You.

So, what is this acronym that makes all the difference in life?

It's SMILE.

SMILE stands for **S**eeing **M**iracles **i**n **L**ife, **E**veryday. Albert Einstein supposedly quipped, "There are two ways to live your life. One is as though nothing is a miracle. The other is as though everything is a miracle." Seeing miracles in everyday life does take training. Life itself is a miracle and a life lived well is miraculous. I make this claim because, as You now know, my own story is miraculous. Imagine going from being fully capable to full paralysis in a few hours as a disease takes over Your body. Then it turns out it's a very rare disease called Guillain-Barré Syndrome, also known as "French Polio." Oh my! Shades of Wilma Rudolph. And also, Elijah. See the miracles, kid. From being able to do everything I wanted in the morning, to the evening where all I could do was move my mouth. That was a miracle. But it seems like it should be a disaster.

Today I'm able to move my arms and somewhat able to move my legs. I can walk a bit with the help of a six-and-half foot walking wand made for me by a Zen master. Still can't walk up a stair or a curb by myself, and I need help twelve hours a day, seven days a week. But I am filled with joy. Why?

Seeing the miracles. Takes me ten minutes to get out of bed in the morning. But I can get out of bed. For years I couldn't.

I can see. I can hear. I have water to drink and food to eat. Family, friends. A place to sleep.

Here is a practice that I want You to try—and it may be a very moving experience. Tonight, when You go to sleep, before You close Your eyes completely, lie on Your back, arms at Your side, fully stretched out and for about eight seconds—no more—just lie there. Breathe gently and imagine that You can't move any part of Your body. Nothing. You can barely speak above a whisper. Can't wiggle Your toes, can't move Your fingers, nothing. And You're going to be like that for a few years.

How are You feeling right now?

Please take a few moments to write down Your thoughts :

_____

_____

_____

_____

_____

Were You scared? Grateful that You can move? Maybe just a bit more appreciative of Your health?

Please make a moment to write here what You feel and think.

So, how does this bit of journaling affect You? Can this kind of "exercise" change You? Unlikely.

What may help are the practices, tips, and tools in this chapter that will let You learn to see miracles in Your everyday life. With these, You'll come to appreciate just how precious an everyday miracle it is to walk, run, jump, skip, and hop.

By doing this work, You are making a difference in Your world and, by extension, creating a ripple effect in the greater world. Yes, that's how important You are. Your speech, Your thoughts, Your deeds all matter. When they align in harmony, You bring benefit to the entire world. You bring life into the world like that of a newborn baby. You bring the miracle. You resonate.

Learning to See

Let's look at something else that is also quite miraculous. You can sit in a chair and speak with someone else while looking into a computer screen. You're able to communicate with people anywhere in the world. Just a very short time ago, that was considered impossible. What is a miracle but the reality of the achievement of the seemingly impossible?

It all depends on how You see. Everyone sees the miracles in different ways. I may see something that You don't see. It does take training. Seeing in this way is an art form.

It is easy to take seeing for granted. One of my dear friends has three children. One day, one of his children woke up and screamed, "I can't see." He became blind overnight from an extremely rare condition. But, here You and I sit, sharing the words of this book between us. Seeing is such a miracle! It is another reason to smile.

A Journal Full of Miracles

Let's now begin the practice of *journaling*.

Please find a notebook or just begin with a piece of paper. Please date it. Label it. Let's label this section, "SMILE."

Here's the practice. For up to three minutes per day (that's the key: a short space of time), write about Your current miracles. It seems that journaling with pen or pencil rather than a mobile device connects pathways in the brain more than typing does. Consciously note miracles that happen within, to, or by Your body. Just a few minutes. You will be using hundreds of billions of brain cells with trillions of connecting synapses traveling at the speed of light. You'll find, experience, and see daily miracles. Once You begin noting the miracles of Your body, You'll improve Your appreciation. And that in turn will enable You to become more empathetic. That's what this practice will give to You.

The first step in any process of growth is to develop conscious awareness. Sometimes it's the only way You can overcome selfishness. When You're able to be consciously aware, You'll avoid situations that have troubled You in the past. You'll learn to say a conscious "yes" or "no." You'll be able to channel Your energy more effectively.

Now, add a note in Your journal describing something miraculous You noticed about Your family. Next about a friend. Both are important to Your ability to live in joy.

Here's a tip: avoid writing a lot one day, then nothing the next. You are building a muscle and a good habit. Don't let a day go by that You didn't journal. Make that commitment to Yourself: never put up a zero. Even if You only write two words, don't let a day go by without a journal entry. Your eyes will be opened. Your heart and mind will be expanded because You are now training Yourself to See Miracles In Life Everyday.

Here's a fun story. My eight-year-old niece recently asked me, "Uncle Barry, can we spell SMILE as SMIEL?"

I thought, why not? They both sound the same. And then I asked her why she would want to do it that way.

She said, "Because then it would mean *Seeing Miracles In Everyday Life.*"

How joyous! Out of the mouth of babes! Please start journaling and enjoying the insights.

Your mind, once stretched by a new idea, never regains its original dimensions.

—*Oliver Wendell Holmes*

Learning to See Differently

Here's a powerful story that I want to share with You. Marcie is a student of mine. Her only son, Dan, is a thirteen-year-old boy with a rare degenerative disease that deteriorates the bones. His life expectancy at this point is about two years and those two years will be a painful process.

Dan's best friend is Jenna, who has the same disease. Jenna's facial features are already deeply distorted, and most people turn away because it's very hard to look at her.

Dan's mother asked him, "Isn't it difficult to look at her?" This thirteen-year-old replied, "Mom, Jenna can't help the way she looks. I have to learn to see differently."

Wow! I have to change the way I see. And then I can see the beauty in the other person. Always.

All that wisdom—and from a thirteen-year-old boy.

The Power of Example

The story of Helen Keller is a key example of the concept of using the SMILE acronym. She was deaf, blind, and unable to speak. Many had given up on her, called her, "addlebrained." But her family cared and found someone named Anne Sullivan to help her. Anne had lived through her own painful situation and cared deeply about Helen. With Anne's patience and insightful techniques, Helen eventually learned to speak, hear, and even to "see"...albeit differently than we do. Helen Keller became one of the most prolific speakers, authors, and champions of life in the past century.

The key thing to remember: example is not the main thing in influencing others; it's the *only* thing! How You live, what You say, what You think all make a difference. When Your thoughts, words, and actions are in harmony, they create such a wondrous "sound" that if You could record it and hear it, You'd be hearing angels singing. This is the true sound of reality. It's who You are. It's in Your ability to SMILE.

We all agree that we are here to build bridges, create relationships, enhance joy, and love. Here's a tool that will bring enormous benefit: think of three people You haven't spoken with in a while. Make a phone call. Reach out; build a bridge. When You're asked why You're calling, reply, "Just to say hello." Just a brief conversation. If need be, leave a voicemail. With Your heart and mind set on building a bridge, You have sent into the world a great power. This will help the "real" You to come out. The positive, purposeful, powerful, pleasant essence of You.

Now do this with three people. Every week. Yes, every week.

Then watch the ripples Your efforts make over the weeks. The months.

The years.

In traffic, You can use the same idea. When someone cuts You off or honks at You, just wave. Why? *Because that is who You are.* You're part of the current of life, the current of love.

Facing the What-Ifs

What if someone says something that You don't like, that offends You? What if it goes against everything You believe in? See what happens if You ask with gentleness, "Why do You think that way or believe that?" You are not here to argue. There is no benefit to anybody in that.

What if You got a flat tire? Well, what if You didn't? What if everything went wonderfully? What would You say? Yeah, "Great, I love it. That's life." Really, what is the difference? I got the job; I didn't get the job. You can fill in the other *what ifs.* Really, what is the difference?

Let's begin to focus on and articulate Your dreams. Dream big dreams. Focus on turning those dreams into goals. And then manifesting them with action. You can do it because You were born to. You're made for this particular period of time. Think about the stories about the people we've met. One woke up blind. Another looks horrible to the world…but to her friend she looks fine.

Learn to SMILE and SMIEL.

> *If one advances confidently in the direction of their dreams, and endeavors to live the life they've imagined, they will meet with success unexpected in common hours.*
>
> —*Henry David Thoreau*

The Takeaways

We are learning to See Miracles In Life Everyday. And In Everyday Life.

Let's grow towards looking at the five different areas where You want to look and find the miracle. These are: Your body, Your family/ friends, Your work, Your finances, and Your thoughts about Yourself.

Use what You have learned wisely. Leverage it, utilize it, journal it. We are learning how to think, reach out, build bridges. Use these practices and encourage others to do the same by example.

We are here for You.

Go forth, live exuberantly. Spread the seeds of joy, happiness, peace, and love.

Growth with Action

List *three* qualities that are miraculous about You .

_____

_____

_____

List *three* qualities that are miraculous about Your family.

_____

_____

_____

List *three* qualities that are miraculous about Your friends.

_____

_____

_____

List *three* qualities that are miraculous about Your body.

_____

_____

_____

List Your *three* Biggest Dreams.

_____

_____

_____

Strategy Two: Happy by Choice: Seeing Life in 3D

Archery range. So read the small sign on Pico Blvd., across from the back lot of the sprawling 20th Century Fox Studios in west Los Angeles. I drove by that sign a dozen times before I finally turned the wheel and decided to follow the arrow. This took me into Rancho Park, an oasis of activities in the midst of the big city. And there it was: an archery range. And there he was: a man for all seasons and for all people.

Francis Peeler: musician, bicyclist, leatherworker, hunter, animal lover, philosopher, friend, archer, and archery teacher par *excellence* who gave free lessons with bows and arrows.

Francis Monroe Peeler was raised by his Aunt Flo in Tuskegee, Alabama, across Franklin Road from Tuskegee Institute, academic home of two black American heroes: George Washington Carver, who lectured and studied there, and Booker T. Washington, the institute's first head.

"When I was five or six, I used to ride on the back of Booker T. Washington's horse," Peeler recalled. "His daughter-in-law was my third-grade teacher.

"In the sixth grade, I carried George Washington Carver's lunches to him. He'd stand at his window and talk to God just like I talk to You."

Peeler stood up, and as he did, it was as if he became George Washington Carver—standing as that pioneer scientist stood more than seven decades ago, staring out the window of his Tuskegee laboratory, holding a branch from a diseased tree. "Now God, You made this tree, You made this branch," intoned Peeler as Carver. "Now—if You will—show me a way to cure it."

The branch was from a peach tree, and Carver found a way to cure the disease, Peeler recalled.

When Peeler was nine, his grandmother taught him to make bows and arrows.

"I cut the willows from the forest and treated them with fire to make bows. The arrows came from reeds I cut in the swamp, and the arrowheads were old Indian arrowheads I found near Euphaupee Creek." Ordinary twine rubbed with beeswax became bow strings.

Kids are the biggest part of Peeler's life. "Kids are home sweet home to me," he said. "They are part of the reason the good Lord put me here. They keep me active, they keep me young, and maybe I keep one or two of them walking on the straight and narrow.

"People say I'm crazy to work here at no pay. I tell them I get paid. Just last week, I got one of the highest paychecks I ever earned.

"There was this boy with cerebral palsy. He kept saying he couldn't shoot. I said, 'Jimmy, you are no longer Jimmy Can't Do It. Now you're Jimmy Can Do It.' Then I spent fifteen minutes putting a bow in his hand, helping him draw and release.

"We shot nine arrows, eight in the target. Then all by himself, he shot three more. Two hit the target, one in the bull's-eye.

"He finished, and said, his voice kind of shaking, 'We did it!'

"I said, 'What did you say?'

"He said it again: 'We did it!'

"I said, 'No, Jimmy, the last three arrows *you* did it.'

"He thought a minute, and gave me a big smile, and he said, 'I did it! I did it!!'

"That's enough pay for me."

And so Francis taught me *how to be happy... by choice*. He said: "Barry Shore. You seem like a smart fella. Let me tell You what I learned from observing people for many decades. These six words will make all the difference in Your life and in the lives of everyone You meet:

"Choice, not chance, determines Your destiny."

And then he said this: "Life is a 3D process: Decision. Discipline. Determination."

Francis embodied all three. And enabled me and countless others to utilize, internalize, and leverage these simple ideas to build a life in JOY.

If You allow circumstances to determine Your mood, then You're not choosing consciously how You feel. When that happens, You're allowing circumstances and people to control what You think and how You act. And *mood* can easily shift to *doom*.

Make a Decision

People are about as happy as they decide to be.

—*Abraham Lincoln*

Happiness is an "inside job." As Viktor Frankl, one of the world's greatest exponents of living life to the full no matter the circumstances, announces in his profound volume, *Yes to Life: In Spite of Everything*, "when the door opens out" is a critical aspect of attaining happiness. We call this service. By recognizing purpose and deciding to live with purpose, one begins to rise above lower SELF and enter the realm of higher SELF.

I have designated the acronym for the lower SELF as: Seeking Excitement, Losing Focus. By avoiding determining a goal or goals, You leave Yourself open to following the call of the senses and find that whatever excites the neurons becomes Your target. You are literally shooting an arrow, drawing the target around wherever the arrow lands, and declaring You hit the bull's-eye.

Sometimes happiness seems as if it's related to excitement or enthusiasm. But those two things are not interchangeable.

What is excitement? Think of a heated pot of water. By putting a flame under the pot, we excite the water to boil. However, once You remove the pot from the flame or reduce the flame, the water returns to its former state. That's excitement. It's a temporary state based upon external circumstances. Once the circumstances change, excitement fades, and then it is extinguished.

On the other hand, there is enthusiasm. The word is based upon the root "thu" which means "God inspired." This is Your internal God-like force. Enthusiasm is constant. It can wax and wane, but an enthusiastic person doesn't allow outside forces to dictate what is inside. So, while excitement is a temporary state, enthusiasm is both internally fed and relies on an infinite source. It's constant.

> *I like to think of the distinction between happiness and joy. Happiness is like rain—it comes from outside circumstances. Joy is an aquifer which is a deep flowing source which can be tapped into despite the circumstances.*
>
> *—Fred Smith*

Enthusiasm is the root of happiness. Therefore, Your baseline is happiness when You identify with enthusiasm. God-like principles don't go away.

Ongoing satisfying and fulfilling happiness happens when the higher SELF is activated. Here SELF becomes the acronym for recognizing that You are a Soul Experiencing Life Fully. Yes, the body and the senses have their place. The ability to tap into deep reservoirs of positive, purposeful, powerful, and pleasant circumstances happens when You can subordinate the senses to the desires of the mind.

Renunciation precedes regeneration. Then *life* flows through Your very being and You can affirm yes to life no matter the circumstances.

One of the results of using these 11 Strategies is to allow Yourself to be a victor, not a victim. You can choose how to respond, not just react, to

Your circumstances. The pause of just a few seconds will allow you to use Your Power Of Thought to reframe Your experience and to choose happiness.

What about being happy by choice? If You can choose to be unhappy, You can choose its opposite. Sad and happy are mirror images, just backwards. Yes, I can choose to be happy, but what about those times when I am naturally sad, like after the passing away of a beloved relative, the loss of a job, the ending of a relationship?

That's the genius of what we are doing. By learning to live in joy or choosing to be happy, You have fewer regrets. You can remember with joy and love, with a smile, the good experiences that You shared. You can understand that this is a process, not an event. So, even choosing to be sad is a temporary diminution of Your normal state of being.

Discipline

True discipline isn't on your back, needling you with imperatives. It's at your side, nudging you with incentives.

—*S. Stanton*

Discipline is the second "D." It has a bad rap because it sounds like a series of imperatives, which narrow instead of expanding consciousness. I prefer to think of it as something or someone near to You who encourages You with incentives. *Discipline* can make you think of disciple. You associate with and become a disciple of the good, because it is what You have decided to do with Your life.

One of my disciplines is swimming. For me, this involved a time-consuming and lengthy process. I essentially had to relearn to swim. I learned to use assistive devices called "floaties" for my legs (so they don't sink) and paddles for my hands (because my fingers don't close). Add in a snorkel, and You have a whole new way to swim. After about a year of practice, I was able to swim a mile continuously. It took ninety-eight minutes, but I did it. A mile without stopping!

The discipline of continuing to swim enlivens my mind and my body. I started swimming a mile twice a week. Then three times. And now, I swim two miles per day, six times a week. Two miles per session. It takes 100 minutes for the two miles. It's truly beautiful what discipline enables. Was it easy? *No!* Was it a straight path? No! Is it worth the ongoing effort? *Yes!*

And this is what has emerged: **Determination**.

> *If you could get up the courage to begin, you have the courage to succeed.*
>
> —D. Viscott

"Courage," wrote Ernest Hemingway, is "grace under pressure." It's true that a diamond is merely common carbon that was subjected to unusual heat and pressure. So it is with the rare being who emerges from overcoming trauma, dealing with toxins, and overturning negative thoughts. Your determination to succeed makes all the difference.

And here is another truism: You cannot fail. As long as You're in the arena, You have the ability to succeed.

It's only over when You quit.

So never quit.

Believe it or not, at this moment, I have swum over 7,951 miles. To put this in perspective: it's swimming form my home in Venice, CA to Hawaii, then over to Fiji and down to Sydney, Australia.

There are a lot of things I can't do. Like walk upstairs by myself, or step up a curb. But I choose to focus on what I can do.

Decision enabled me to begin. *Discipline* has given me the perspective, and *determination* has yielded great results.

You can see why these are a vital part of joy.

I urge You to risk being happy! Risk being enthusiastic, knowing that enthusiasm stands for Your internal God-like quality. It is that quality which will enable You to live in and become a FOG: Fountain Of Goodness. Take the risk of being the victor and not the victim. The word victim leaves Your vocabulary when You choose happiness. You will make the quantum leap into happiness, not in the mood but in the mode.

We see therefore that life is a 3D process. Only two dimensions exist on paper, with straight lines that lie flat. Then the third dimension pops off the plane and the picture becomes alive.

When we live by choosing happiness, we utilize the 3Ds: Decision, Discipline, and Determination. *Decision* means that as a conscious person, You have made the conscious choice to live in the world of happiness. Science demonstrates that this alone, *deciding*, changes Your physiology, changes Your demeanor—in fact changes Your entire outlook on life. You're no longer subject to or dominated by outside circumstances, or outside events. You have decided to live in joy!

Meditation…and Pressing "Pause" on Anger

Look at the word *medication*. Let's replace the "c" with a "t" and You now have *meditation*. Again, words are important. The best meditation is, in my opinion, medication. Meditation centered upon divine realities is the very essence and soul of prayer. It is the silent reaching upward of the soul toward the eternal.

And the best medication is meditation. Meditation can help You because when You are in joy, everyone around You feels it—You exude it. This is the essence of good HEALTH: Helping Everyone Achieve Life Through Happiness. You can meditate in as little as two minutes. Do it once before noon and once after noon. You'll be amazed at the benefits (see https://www.barryshore.com/94seconds/).

Now let's look at the opposite side of the spectrum. What is it that ruins or diminishes happiness? Anger. Rage. Upset. When we forget the good, anger can enter and we put our happiness and that of others in danger. The key difference is the power of thought.

For instance, anger can be used constructively sometimes. Think of a child running into the street to fetch his or her ball. Would You yell at this child to get him or her out of danger? Of course! You care about the child, so You would raise Your voice in this situation. But here's the key:

that is feigned anger, which You'd use selectively and for a purpose. This is because it's applied with awareness and intention.

But when anger is allowed to become rage, it's no longer a conscious decision, it's a blind reaction and usually causes strife, which is a rift between people. The time-tested process of counting to five or ten (or, in some cases, twenty!) allows the requisite distance between circumstance and response to decide how and what to do. These precious moments can save Your happiness.

The Takeaways

Life is a 3D process

Decision. Discipline. Determination.

The six most important words to know:

Choice, not chance, determines your destiny.

You're a disciplined person leading a determined life.

You are continually reinforcing what You are learning because You have discovered the secret and power of everyday words and terms.

Happiness is embodied in ever striving forward.

Growth with Action: Utilizing the 3Ds in Your Life

Write down three decisions that You have made or will make in the next three days to further Your goal/s .

_____

_____

_____

Write down three actions/disciplines that You are currently using or will use in the next three days to further your goal/s.

_____

_____

_____

Write Your three main determinations that are inviolable for You in relation to Your goal/s.

_____

_____

_____

Write down three situations that have occurred in the past three months that have tested Your discipline and determination.

_____

_____

_____

Write down how You handled each one.

_____

_____

_____

Strategy Three: Use Your Power: Express!

"What a rotten day."

It was deep dark December in Boston, Massachusetts, at around 11:30 a.m. Outside was bone-chilling cold and snow mixed with rain—we called it sleet. Couldn't go out sledding or build a snowman or even make snowballs. Just "rotten." I was an eight-year-old boy staring out the window and bemoaning the weather and my life.

And then I heard, "What did You say, Bearshie?" My beloved aunt's nickname for me. *What did You say*? Before I could even mouth a word, Auntie Edie began explaining and extolling the benefits of rain, snow, winter, and the forthcoming buds and growth that would emerge from all the nutrients of water currently saturating the earth.

I really had no idea what she was saying; but she said it with such a verve and smile and *love* that I began squinting—trying to make sure that she was seeing the same world I was looking at.

But then, as I listened, everything flipped. *I* started to see what *she* saw.

And the way I learned to see that day changed my life.

Did I ever complain again? Certainly. I'm human. Did I hesitate to complain? Yes. And did I eventually stop complaining by the ripe old age of sixteen? Again, yes.

Because I was blessed to have someone I loved and trusted show me another way. And the result of that one afternoon enabled me to meet various challenges, from relatively small to gigantic, with a new sensibility.

If there is a "strategy" in life that will propel You forward with a lightness of spirit it is this: *Don't Complain.*

And its companion: *Don't Blame.*

From the wisdom literature of past millennia:

> *Of what shall a living person complain?*
>
> —*Lamentations 3:39*

How subtle, simple, profound. If one is alive, of what is there to complain?

The great story of Jonah contains several unique references to harrowing experiences, but the one toward the end of the book is of interest here. Jonah completes his task of warning the people of a major metropolitan city to examine their ways and change for the better. They do so. Jonah then leaves and sits outside the city, somewhat forlorn.

He's tired, hungry, and confused. God causes a tree with nourishing fruit to spring up and Jonah is sated and shaded from the blistering sun. Then the tree dies. Jonah is forlorn.

Then God asks, Why are You downcast? The tree—which You had no hand in propagating—came quickly, fed You, and then it left. Such is life. Be appreciative for what You have when You have it. Don't look to complain or blame. No one knows what the morrow will bring.

The Present Time

As I write, we have just experienced what I deem the "100 days that shook the world." From mid-March 2020 until the end of June 2020, the United States has shifted from the world's most successful economy in history to an almost complete shutdown.

Covid-19, originating in China, became a worldwide pandemic. The result was panic and tragedy for almost every nation. In the USA, millions of businesses were closed down, tens of millions of people were out of work, unique measures were imposed upon the populace, families were in turmoil, schools were closed, shock and dismay were felt throughout the country.

How could one not complain? How could one not blame?

It might seem almost "natural" to do so. Yes, it might. Unless You were trained or in training to see beyond the immediate and recognize that the ability to be present and live in the now could reduce, mitigate, maybe even eliminate the panic—and certainly could eliminate the anger and STRESS of this new reality.

This strategy moves us closer to living in JOY. Daily. To review: we have three techniques that underlie all our work: life has purpose; go MAD (Make A Difference); and unlock the secrets of everyday words and terms by transforming them into powerful positive acronyms that yield guidance and support.

Most people know intellectually that blaming or complaining are not beneficial. But the question is *why*.

Or rather, why not?

My Auntie Edie explained to me later in life that the negativity that emanates from Your mind and then Your speech is so toxic that it's like an acid eating at Your very essence. Who wants that? And as we think about the reality of complaining and blaming, it's easy to recognize the truth of that insight: we all know people who have been eaten away inside by their habitual complaints, by their refusal to take responsibility.

Jocko Willink, in his bestselling book *Extreme Ownership*, delineates the various aspects of learning to accept, recognize, and utilize the core quality of *responsibility*. Personal responsibility, to the level of 100%, is not only an attribute that can be learned, but is foundational to a successful business, home, and life.

Therefore, the twin traits of *don't complain* and *don't blame* are essential qualities in living successfully and therefore in JOY.

This is true under all circumstances and through all vicissitudes.

Speech: The Power of Thought, Channeled out into the World

Over the years, I have found that the best way of learning to let go of complaining and blaming is to become a "POT" advocate. We're using this acronym for Power Of Thought. It's in Your power to change Your thoughts about Your circumstances by reframing. Much as happened for me as an eight-year-old, staring out the window at that snowy, sleety winter's day.

We know that our thoughts can give rise to our words, which in turn influence our deeds. Here's the insight I was taught: Speech is the vessel that channels blessing into the world and I, as a conscious, conscientious person, try with all of my faculties to continually dispense blessing.

Speech, therefore, is either a vessel for the negative or for the positive. We can't hold both at the same time. They are incompatible. We need to choose. By choosing to use the positive, and by doing so consciously and continually, You are programming (aka NLP: neural linguistic programming) Yourself and producing the benefits that accrue to thinking, speaking, and doing the positive.

Try saying, "Good job." Or, "That was well done." Or even something as simple as, "Hi, nice to see You."

Complaining and casting blame causes us to rot from the inside, as we gather stress and our systems break down. This resembles the process of rust. *Rust* and *rot* are similar words. When You act in a way that is destructive of others or Yourself, You begin the process of internal rot. It's so harmful because it seems to attack the other person, yet it really eats at us.

Accountability is hard. Blame is easy. One builds trust, the other destroys it.

—*Simon Sinek*

We often go through our days by rote, doing the same thing over and over. Words matter, even letters matter. If You subtract the "e" from rote, You have rot. Unconsciously, a person encourages the formation of rot within because he or she accepts and expresses, often without thinking, the blame or complaint that created the disturbance or rot in the first place.

On the other hand, when You embrace the positive You allow yourself to flow. Without those things that are causing You to feel bad about Yourself or others, You can let go and embrace the joy within. Effort-free flow is reflected as Your greatness. Just like a champion athlete, Your flow appears effortless. And just like a skilled athlete, it does take training, determination, and practice to achieve the flow.

The ABCs of Flow

As a means toward getting into that flow, consider the letters "ABC." Again, we can turn the most common expression into something we can leverage for our benefit. First thing in the morning, before getting out of bed, say Your "ABCs." Say and imagine Yourself with **A**bundance, **B**ounty, and **C**hanneling of good.

I have used this expression so that I could get my feet out of bed—and for me, there were *years* when that was a nearly impossible task. Using this expression, I imagined myself as channeling abundance, bounty, and goodness. Even while paralyzed. So there is no limit to what You can achieve with this thought. You can't hold the incompatible thought of a complaint or blame. You can create a place in Your mind where blame and complaint cannot dwell.

You might prefer, "I am healthy, I am wealthy, I am wise." Use whatever short phrase will enable You to replace negativity and enjoy Your movement toward the joy that You are creating.

When we use simple words and remember the truths taught by our daily use of positive acronyms, there is no room or need for complaining. If You begin to complain, You will quickly recognize this, and change Your thought and behavior patterns. It's the beauty of the system. It works with Your thought *until the subconscious becomes the conscious*. You will not need to seek joy; it will be Yours automatically.

Facing Difficulty—and Transforming It

Let's also acknowledge that there are difficult—if not absolutely devastating—situations that do exist. This strategy is not designed to have anyone deny reality. It is the essence of living and being human to recognize what things can be changed. What things need to be accepted. And to have the courage and wisdom to know the difference.

Devastation, whether wrought by natural disasters, evil actors/actions, and one's own inattention do occur. The issue at hand is: what is Your response?

Looking back inside ourselves can help us to have what is called "enlightened self-interest." It is enlightened because it is from a higher self or God, and it is self-interest because it serves us and all who interact with us.

I continually remind myself and those I am privileged to work with that speech is the vessel that channels blessings into the world. I was fortunate to meet a famous author who coined the phrase "conscious capitalism." It would seem to be an oxymoron, but he combines those elements of the best of capitalism and consciousness. In this view, people are the greatest asset in any organization. A positive view, indeed! We can bring our awareness to focus on the good of all which is in the end what capitalism promises. That is our consciousness. We can be grateful to participate in such a bounteous system.

Finding JOY at Work

While on the topic of capitalism and money, let's look at the way most of us make money—let's look at what we do when we go to work.

Consider the popular saying, "TGIF" (or "Thank God It's Friday"). If we think about it, we'll see this is based upon the negative idea that the work week was/is difficult and that we're glad it's over. A little like a complaint, don't You think?

What about shifting that acronym around? Let's try saying, "TGIM!" (or "Thank Goodness It's Monday!"). You can easily see how that sets us up for a great week. Again, *always use Your language to Your advantage*.

Here's another acronym—one that a friend taught me—and it will help You reorient Your perception of the workday: TGIT. Meaning, "Thank God It's Today!"

All these small changes in our thinking will add up to a shift in our capacity to perform at our best, to improve our lot, and to grow healthier, wealthier, and wiser.

And while on the topic of work, let's move to the idea of JAWS: Joy At Work Sessions. This is a highly interactive program taught by Larry Bradley and me, and it's aimed at businesses that want to encourage their most precious assets: their people.[4]

Larry is a highly regarded executive and a pension administrator of one of the largest unions in the world. JAWS was started as the means to build a Conscious Happiness Practice (CHP). Whether someone is working at home or in the in-person environment of an office, the dynamics of professional relationships have largely been unchanged. Currently such issues as "absenteeism" and "non-presenteeism" are a *trillion*-dollar cost problem to U.S. business. One of the most effective ways of lowering this huge and growing waste is to counter it with the positive, purposeful attributes that the work environment can provide. The cure is not beyond the reach of business once the diagnosis is made and accepted.

Facing the Consequences—and the Consequences are Good

One of the powerful corollaries of working and living in JOY is the knowledge that You cannot fail. I'm going to repeat that: You cannot fail when You work in the world as though You are a blessing. When You use blessings in Your thoughts and speech, they will come back to You. It's a law of the universe. Law is often heard as a harsh word. In our world, LAW stands for **L**ove **A**nd **W**isdom. Your movement toward success is a LAW. It is consequential.

"But Barry," You might say, "I'd like to believe that the world is based on justice, not injustice, built on order not chaos, but it doesn't appear that way. Not to me."

Success is simple. What does that mean? It means that it takes work— work in the truest sense of the word. It means effort on all levels as Your thoughts, words, and actions all work together. You are the dynamic. Your work, and the goodness that You spread, will enable the world to work better, to love more, and will inspire people to live healthier, wealthier, and wiser lives. You will grow to see the order of the world and recognize the sense of justice that good living brings.

---

4   See www.joyatworksessions.com.

Ever hear of Michelangelo? Of course! Here's a quote attributed to him that animates all who use it:

> *The danger for most of us is not that our aim is too high and that we miss it, it's that it's too low and that we achieve it.*

Your flow comes from Your vision. You are in this process all the time. When You repeat the same bad behavior over and over it's because You are caught in the drain/stagnation. Addiction is getting caught in the negative cycle, shooting too low, not realizing that You can change Your circumstance by changing Your thinking. It's forgetting that You can Make A Difference. Once You begin to strive to be the best possible You, things will change in amazing ways.

When You assume responsibility for Your thoughts, words, and deeds, You relieve Yourself of the burden of carrying blame. Blame is a heavy load. And sometimes the blame is even justified. Yes, someone actually planned to do You harm. And carried it out. Yes, it hurts. Yes, it caused loss. At some point You sit, think, examine, and ask: am I better for carrying this anger? This rage? This blame? It's unlikely the answer is yes. By letting go and figuratively placing the load of blame in a space, looking at it, and walking away, You can liberate Yourself and begin to live in joy.

It's Your choice.

And that's the heart of this powerful strategy.

Don't complain. Don't blame.

Letting Go of the Burden of Blame

You can live the life that You want. Don't sigh, "If only." Smile and sing out: "*Yes!*"

Think of complaint or blame like this. You are out in a boat in the ocean, but You forgot Your water bottle. Thirsty, You dip a cup into the ocean. You drink some of the salty water. You think You are satisfying your desire, but really, in just a moment, You'll be thirstier, You'll want more. Eventually, the salt water will overload Your kidneys and will kill You.

Blame is like that: it rots the inside, making You think that if You search for more blame that it'll help. But the truth is that blame, like the saltwater, will make You want more and more, and eventually Your system will stagnate and You will die—inside if not outside.

In every situation, You have a choice about how You will respond. Even in times when You find someone has violated Your trust, You can complain, and blame, but like drinking the seawater, it will make You seek to blame and complain more and more, and You will turn from being a fountain of positivity to becoming a drain on Yourself and all around You. It's Your choice.

Becoming a Fountain of JOY

When You resolve to take positive action, You move into growth mode. This is especially important in the morning and when You go to sleep in the evening. We can enter sleep consciously by choosing concepts of appreciation. If we focus on these when we are on the verge of sleeping, we will wake up with appreciation for our day. Again, You can use the mantra of ABC. **A**bundance, **B**ounty, and **C**hanneling of good.

It takes less than sixty seconds of easy effort.

To reinforce Your practice of being a channel of goodness, begin with Verbalize, Visualize and Emotionalize (VVE). With deep emotion, visualize certain people that You want to send loving energy to. And verbalize the loving, positive message. It won't matter if they hear You or not, they will feel Your positive energy. Use this as well as Your "ABCs." Do these for sixty seconds first thing in the morning—before checking Your cell phone, getting coffee, or doing any other activity.

Do these and You will live in and be a FOG: a **F**ountain **O**f **G**oodness. You will bring that bubbling sense of goodness along with you, channeling prosperity, health, and wisdom to light the world. Believe me, the world needs You! Especially now. Keep in mind the thought from Michelangelo—dream big, set goals to hit that are more than You thought You could do, and don't settle for what is easy.

The Takeaways

Your thoughts determine Your attitude.

Don't complain and don't blame are ideas that You can control.

Say and internalize: TGIT.

Learn to use ABC.....VVE.

You're either a Fountain or a Drain. Your choice.

Growth with Action:

Write three things that cause You to complain .

_____

_____

_____

Write three times in the past thirty days that You blamed someone for something.

_____

_____

_____

Write two things that You can do in the next twenty-four hours to help You stop complaining about one of the items above.

_____

_____

_____

Write two things You can do over the next week to stop You from blaming someone else when something You don't like happens.

_____

_____

_____

Strategy Four: How to Be Emotionally Bullet-proof

"Great move, Shore...you might make a good wrestler someday. Maybe even competition level."

After hearing that, my head was so swollen that I could barely fit through the door to the locker room. Mr. Marsh was not given to easy compliments. And I was working really hard and wanted to do well.

So, it was especially galling when, a few weeks later at state high school meet, I bombed out and made some really bogus moves that lost me and the team a berth in the next round. And were my teammates understanding? No way. Did the coach give me a pep talk about "hey, next time, champ"? No way. First of all, there was no next time—this was senior year. And secondly...I *did* mess up.

It was then that the words of Mr. Campbell, my math tutor, came into my mind: "If You let compliments go to Your head, You'll let complaints go to Your heart."

Treating Both Compliments and Complaints the Same

In this segment, we're going to be working with one of the most important strategies for reclaiming Your essence: *Don't take anything personally*.

One of the most natural responses to anything adverse that happens is to face it like it's a personal attack. But with the maturity You are developing and the ways of thinking You're committing to, You'll be able to work with Your problems and concerns in a new way.

Why? Because You will create the ability to look candidly at Yourself.

You will learn how to look at Yourself in the light of the truth and the result will be that You will not feel attacked in Your interactions with family, friends, teachers, classmates. When You use this chapter's strategy effectively, You will have better interactions in any and all of Your relationships. You will be able to recognize who You are in the midst of them.

You will see clearly because You will never take anything personally.

Even when it *is* meant to You personally.

How this Strategy Works Together with All the Others

One of the benefits of these 11 Strategies is that they're part of a tapestry that's woven together. When we integrate the strategies, they form a new way for us to think about and understand our world. This integrative approach enables us to recast or reframe incidences into positive, purposeful, powerful ones that will yield as-yet-unseen benefits.

Remember, by leveraging the three fundamentals, You are creating a new life. Your life is purposeful. You can go MAD: Make A Difference. And You can unlock the power of everyday words and terms.

All three fundamentals interweave with all 11 Strategies. But that last fundamental is especially important for our current strategy of *don't take it personally*. Play with words that You consider insulting and build positive, pleasant acronyms with them. The result is that words and epithets hurled at You to destroy You become like marshmallows because You diffused them and suffused them with Your life force. There is nothing more powerful than this.

Remember, if You do take things personally, then You let outside forces dictate Your mood, Your outlook, and eventually Your performance. Words are important, but You determine their shape and meaning. Indeed, when You let others control Your mood by their speech and actions, You are inviting doom.

What if doom hits you like a brick? Health psychologist and founder of Emotional Brain Training (EBT) Laurel Mellin discovered a way to transform those toxic emotions into joy, just by expressing your feelings. In her latest book, The Stress Solution, the New York Times bestselling author shows how to turn anxiety, depression, hostility and shame into joy. You begin by expressing your negative feelings as that releases stress. Then positive emotions – feeling grateful, happy, secure and proud – start flowing.

What is the beautiful message here? Underneath those toxic negative emotions is JOY. Suppressing feelings can cause them to go underground and produce more stress. However, releasing them in this special way makes it easier to change your perspective, which is essential.

Changing Your Perspective

Most of the people You will meet in life aren't always happy. But when You recognize there is a simple mood shift available and You control it, then You are no longer subject to the moods of others. Their shifting mood stops being personal, which allows You to live in a state of joy no matter what is happening. You become able to live as You want to no matter what those around You are feeling or thinking. Not that You are uncaring, it's just that You realize it's not personal.

One great revelation that You have as You age is realizing that no one is really thinking about You. I'll say it again: No one is really thinking about You. There's a famous meme that says that when You're twenty, You care what everyone thinks; when You're forty, You stop caring what everyone thinks; and when You're sixty, You realize no one was thinking about You in the first place.

You can let compliments go, You can let insults pass You by, because You know that it is not really about You, anyway. What freedom! It's like having clear goggles when You swim. You want to keep them clean, just as in Your life You want to clear away what others think of You. This will allow You to enjoy the clarity and wonder of the joy that You create.

Let's keep those googles clean. Here's a practical way: use Your journal. Try to note two positive events every day. Just two. Everyday.

Refusing to Live a LIE—and Other Helpful Words

Another acronym that can help us to use this strategy and to remember to let things go is LIE—which stands for **Life-Inhibiting Experience**. We don't engage in lies because they inhibit our life—and why would we want to inhibit our lives in the first place? That's the opposite of joy.

By reprogramming our minds to become aware of our words, we lay down new tracks for our thinking. NLP is the technical term: Neuro Linguistic Programming. So, let's begin our NLP as we move through all of these strategies and understand that everything we talk about, everything we note in our journals and in our expression, is geared toward making sure that we live in joy, daily.

JOG a while—in our new world we're building together, that stands for **Joy Of Giving**. Generosity is central to the act of living in JOY and You can easily understand why. Giving unlocks the portal through which You connect with others. It affirms Your connection to others and it feels good. By connecting in this way, it is inevitable that You will receive in far greater measure than what You give.

Some may say, "But You've never been subjected to what I've experienced, Mr. Shore."

I'll respond to that by saying I'm here to help You become a POT HEAD: **Power Of Thought, Helping Everyone Achieve Destiny**. It's in our power to remember that nothing is really about us. It never was. No matter what it was, we were not the target.

Remember, the word *no* has the same sound as the word *know*. People often hear the word *no*. But *no* is missing two key letters: that is, "K" and "W." Many people will take the word *no* to mean rejection, but if they add the "K" and "W," they can gain a far different and deeper meaning. The "K" stands for *kindness* and "W" stands for *wisdom*. This simple and effective way of reprogramming the mind unlocks positivity and helps us along the way to joy!

Chance does not dictate how Your life unfolds, rather it unfolds the way You think about the events in Your life. "No" isn't always personal, and even if it was, it can be a key to unlocking the kind and the wise in any situation. "No" can be the opening of a bright world of possibility as You respond to Your circumstances with kindness, and as You gain the wisdom to choose Your destiny.

A great sage spoke of two kinds of sorrow and two kinds of joy. He said that if a person broods over the misfortunes that have come upon them and despairs of any hope, that's the type of sorrow that's debilitating. The divine presence doesn't visit there. It doesn't reside in dejection and despair. The other type of sorrow is practiced by someone who looks, examines, and recognizes what they lack and is willing to make the effort to change. Hope comes and uplifts.

There are also two kinds of joy. There's the joy of the person filled with excitement at empty and foolish pleasures devoid of inner substance. You can call that merrymaking for the sake of merrymaking. On the other hand, substantive joy doesn't recognize lack or try to fill a hole. It's more like a truly joyful person whose house has burned down, but who sees the opportunity to build anew. With every brick or stone that he lays, he feels a deep joy within his heart.

Joy calms the senses and fills the heart with might and power. The **P**ower **O**f **P**rayer is a member of this family because he's POP. Rather than dwell in what he doesn't have, he takes his silent prayer for renewal and builds his house.

Some other powerful ways to think of POP are **P**ower **O**f **P**atience and the **P**ower **O**f **P**urpose. You can see each of these in our example of the person who rebuilds their house. They are patient enough to step back and see the big picture, and purposeful enough to know that anything destroyed can be rebuilt with some effort.

As You mature and deepen Your understanding of Yourself, You begin to recognize that the world is here for one reason only: to give and receive joy. It's a 3D process: making a *decision* to live positively, having the *discipline* to follow through, and having the *determination* to live that way no matter the obstacles.

You have in this way freed Yourself from "taking things personally."

You have become the master of Your universe.

The Takeaways

If You let compliments go to Your head, You'll let complaints go to Your heart.

Don't allow insults to control Your mood.

Don't let a LIE in.

Learn to surround NO with K and W.

Become a POT HEAD.

Growth with Action

Enter two positive events You saw in Your Journal—every day .

_____

_____

_____

_____

Note two times this week when You heard NO and were are able to surround it with K and W .

_____

_____

_____

_____

Write about a time when you were able to laugh inwardly as You were either complimented or disparaged .

_____

_____

_____

_____

Strategy Five: The Power of a Few Good Words

Terrible T wants to see me? Oh no! What could this be about?

Mrs. Thompson was the principal of our school and had a notorious reputation as a fire-breathing dragon.

And that was on a good day.

So being called into her office wasn't promising.

"Barry Shore," she greeted me as I entered. "Good. Sit down please. Let's discuss Your graduation speech."

As class president, I thought my role was about school dances, having fun, and being thirteen. But from Mrs. T's perspective, apparently, what was important was the two speeches I was going to give: one at the science fair and one at the commencement at year's end.

My stomach tensed and twisted. Speaking in public was *not* something I wanted to do.

But before I could protest, Mrs. T asked me if I knew the Gettysburg Address. Well of course I knew of it.

No. She meant did I *know* it...by heart. Memorized.

No.

She said, "You mean, 'not yet.' Please be here at the same time next week and recite it for me." Then she said, "Thank You."

This was 1961. Authority spoke. I was dismissed.

And so began the most important process for success in my life. Mrs. T. taught me this vital lesson: *Your words matter.* The important thing was to express, not impress.

My recitation of the Gettysburg Address went less than well—that first time. Amazingly, Mrs. T made the time and effort to work with me and instilled in me the confidence that enabled me to express ideas and connect one-on-one with any audience, no matter its size.

That confidence stayed with me for the rest of my life. Thank You, Mrs. T.

Your words matter. Which words You say. When You say them.

And how You say them matters too. Used correctly in a positive, purposeful, powerful, and pleasant way, words can create more harmony, peace, love, happiness, and joy in the world. And of course, the opposite is equally true: wield them to rile and rouse anger and hate, and the world can be devastated.

> *Life and Death are in the hands of the tongue.*
>
> —*Proverbs 18:21*

Ancient wisdom is not just old; it lasts because it's inherently true. Therefore, unlocking the secrets and the power of everyday words and terms makes a difference in life.

The Tools of Our Trade

Let's look at the word, words. Your words matter because it is words we use to paint pictures, create images, and tell stories. By moving the letter "S" in *words* we can make a *sword*. The sword can cut, stab, or defend. It can cut through many things including the human body. We have to be careful how we wield our sword, and how we wield our words, because the same sword that can cause tremendous harm can also unleash enormous benefit, if used correctly. Think of a small sword we term a "scalpel." Death and life are in the power of the tongue. Not the gun, not the sword, not the bomb, but the tongue. Our words can heal or hurt.

But what about "sticks and stones may break my bones, but words can never harm me"? It's true—to an extent. I personally prefer hurled epithets to inflexible heavy objects.

And as we learned in the strategy titled, "don't take it personally," there is an important skill in learning to handle harmful words with a calm, aware mind. The harm and the charm of words is powerful—but they have power only in so far as You allow them to.

We can take the words that are said to us, whether negatively or positively, and brush them aside. But when it comes to this strategy, we are focused on the words that come from our own lips. We want our words to be the sort that are *not* easily brushed aside. We also want to make them powerful, purposeful, positive, and pleasant as possible because we don't know where our words will travel, but wherever they *do* travel, we want the effect they have on others to be beneficial. Small things like words can add up to be big consequences. In science that's known as "The Butterfly Effect." [5]

Becoming One Who Blesses

My father was a quiet, almost stoic, man. We rarely interacted except when we went to the Russian steam bath together on Sunday mornings—leaving the house at 5 a.m.! On those sleepy drives, he would always warn me and urge me to be conscious of what I say with this phrase: If You don't have something nice to say, don't say anything. He himself exemplified this.

Decades later, I learned this folksy advice in a more sophisticated embodiment from a revered teacher, who was ninety-one when I learned with him. He often repeated: *Speech is the vessel that channels blessing into the world, and I, as a conscious, conscientious being, continually dispense blessing.* "Well done"; "Good job"; "You look great today"; "Nice"; "Thank You." Literally and figuratively, You can use Your vocabulary to bring the world tremendous benefit. When we walked together, this teacher of mine would quietly bless people in their homes. His whole being was as a channel of goodness. And he lived healthfully until the age of 105, despite seeing many tragedies. And he left this world peacefully.

---

5   The Butterfly Effect metaphor is simply meant to demonstrate that small, seemingly insignificant events can lead to significant results over time. To put it another way, small variances in initial conditions can have profound and widely divergent effects on a system. Such chaotic systems are unpredictable by their very nature.

Decide to become a thanking, thinking being. Today. From now forward. For the rest of Your life. Envision Yourself as a channel of goodness. And that the world is depending upon You to be so. Onerous? More like an honor!

Congratulations.

Positive, purposeful, powerful, pleasant words create a ripple effect in the world. Those who You thank appreciate it, even if they do not respond. Your words transcend both time and space, because they tap into the universal FLOW of Fantastic Love-Oriented Words.

Cultivating a Habit of Gratitude

Now, You are ready to become a professional "thanker": someone who lives life on a higher plane. Your aspiration is to become the *best possible* You. If You want to get to this level, You can—and should!—train Yourself to say "thank You" at least three times a day.

Do this consciously and conscientiously. You want it to be real. So real that it becomes part and parcel of Your very essence.

Just remember how powerful Your words are.

Here's a practice that may help. For three days, notice every time You use one of the common "placeholder" phrases. These are frequently used words that don't enhance Your being. It might be "no problem." Or hesitations like "um." Or maybe You use placeholders such as "You know" or "like."

To help You, ask a trusted friend to let You know when You use the phrase. The key is to become more aware of what You say habitually.

Once You find Your "non-thinking" phrase/words, consider eliminating or at least reducing their use for three days in a row. Funnily enough, it's not easy.

Here's a suggestion that has proven beneficial for me and a number of my students. Once You've identified Your "non-thinking" or placeholder phrase, adopt a replacement phrase that is positive and resonates with You.

For instance, one friend says "Thank You, dear LORD"; another uses *"fantabulous."* The result is a highly sensitized awareness and a newfound respect for what You say—and even more importantly, how You think. This exercise is so powerful that You can use it to transform Your speech patterns and, in the course of time (in my experience, usually 90-120 days), You'll feel a renewed ability to use uplifting, pleasant, encouraging words. They'll flow more readily, and You'll become the channel of blessing. How fun is that!

Words Open the Way to Knowledge

Here's a simple story. When my son was very young, we'd go on walks. I'd ask him, "What do You see?" He said, "The sun." I said, "Great. Where are the stars?" He said, "It's daytime, Papa. They only come out at night." I asked him, "But the sun doesn't go away then, only then we can't see it." He looked at me. Eventually he learned and laughed when he was able to tell me that the stars are always there, and the sun was too, but that the earth is spinning and rotating in an orbit. Words stimulate, and curiosity is peaked.

Words matter. For example, even such simple mundane expressions as "sunrise" and "sunset" belie the reality. They describe only what we humans can see. The sun never rises or sets. It's only that we can't see it all the time. Walking at night with my son, I began talking about the number of stars, and I told him that there were vast numbers of them, and most were as large as our world. And bigger. His eyes widened.

The point for us as conscious beings is that the stars are always there, sometimes they're just hidden, and the same thing for the sun. Many things which we depend upon and hail as truth are actually hidden from us. Thus, the acronym for truth: **T**otal **R**eliance **U**pon **T**he **H**idden.

Talking to Yourself

A number of years ago, I was standing up in the morning, moving around freely. By the evening I was in the hospital, paralyzed from my neck down. It was not from a spinal injury or car accident, rather from a rare disease. Thankfully, almost two decades later, I can move my arms and my upper body. I still can't stand on my own. I can't stand still without support. But with the help of a six-and-a-half foot walking wand, I am ambulatory!

My words—my SELF TALK—mattered throughout the process. They enabled me to envision sitting up in bed. Turning over by myself. Putting my feet over the side of the bed. Being vertical. Being ambulatory.

That's why I define SELF TALK as recognizing that You are a **S**oul **E**xperiencing **L**ife **F**ully, **T**eaching **A**lways **L**ove & **K**indness.

Think of how You would listen to and comfort a close friend or relative who needed Your help and insight. You would listen carefully and not dismiss the person with "it will all be fine." What You would do is to think of how You could help and then You would do everything You could to teach/help always with love and kindness.

How much more so for oneself?

Your Name: A Word that Matters

Words are the bridge that connect the human and the divine. Here's an example from the lowly cow, the animal whose very essence is to give nourishment. Let's be a COW, a **C**hooser **O**f **W**ords, a giver.

What's the best way to give someone else "nourishment"? Use their name. This is the sweetest sound a human can hear. Note the next time You're in a crowded room, and someone calls Your name. You feel it, You hear it. They may not even be calling You. Maybe another has Your same name. It didn't matter. The fact is that Your name sounds sweet. Now think of how sweet it is when called by someone You care about. Ah, life!

As a COW, I'm going to tell You a little story about a name. Through years of aquatic therapy to help relieve my paralysis, I was able to move my arms and my legs. In time and with perseverance, I learned to swim again.

When I finish my swim, I'm able to get myself to the edge of the pool and push myself up onto the ledge and from there to push myself, with help, onto a chair. One day, after I'd done this, a boy coming my way stopped and asked, "Do You need some help?"

How wondrous! I didn't want to say no, so I said, "That's so nice of You. Thank You. I don't need help but thank You for asking." Then I asked his name.

He was hesitant but said, "Lucien."

I said, "Lucien, I just want to tell You how much I appreciate that You asked me if I needed help. Lucien, here are some Keep Smiling cards. Please give them to people You love and keep one for Yourself. Thank You, Lucien."

He beamed.

I was buoyed with hope. A ten-year-old boy stops and asks this elderly person, "How can I help You?" In my opinion, these are the five most important words a person can say on a regular basis.

Several hours earlier, I came to the aquatic center. I was walking with my wand and approaching me was this wondrous being in a wheelchair. I know her. She's Aida. Aida is 108 years....old? She goes to the pool three to four times a week, and she walks in the water in a lane just for people with special needs. I swim with her in that lane. I swim while she's walking. The point is, she's an inspiration. As we pass, she says, "Hi Barry. Sing me a song." At 108, she remembers my name! And I sing to her...and she hums along. With a bright smile.

It's a great day, seeing Aida, and hearing my name, and experiencing Lucien who asked me those famous five words, "How can I help You?"

Your words matter!

Words, the Makers of Worlds

As noted above, the most powerful way in which Your words matter is self-talk. Numerous studies have shown that the words You use when speaking to Yourself are the most important words You hear. When You make Your words into aspirations, they inspire You. This is a two-step process that is completely within Your control. Avoid negative words/terms. Use positive, purposeful, uplifting terms. Under all circumstances.

Think about top athletes and competitors in any field. The game, business, process is won in the mind, often before the actual event! It's the envisioning process that enables success. You are the maker and shaper of Your character and Your being.

Once You recognize the deep truth of this, You are free to begin the process and build Your self-talk "muscles." Your words are now a matter of choice, not chance. And as You use Your words with purpose, You internalize the six most important words for Your life: *choice, not chance, determines Your destiny*. You take the world as it is and choose the narrative that serves You. You move away from the LIE (life-inhibiting experience) that the world controls You.

Recently the Pope was speaking in Italy and began chastising members of the Cosa Nostra (mafia) by telling them that they're going to that place that doesn't have harps and angels singing. He wasn't coddling them; he was speaking truth. It's up to You individually to integrate this remarkable power of Your words so that You can use it to shape and mold who You are—and so You can have a positive influence on the world around You. The result of the Pope's words there? One of the more well-known leaders of the mafia decided to begin repentance.

Your thinking journal helps You become a dispenser in the world of blessing speech. Start today. Right now. Resolve to be disciplined and determined to care for Yourself three times a day. Gradually Your speaking muscles will be so positive, purposeful, and powerful that You'll become a professional blessing dispenser. And the result? You will be healthier. Wealthier. Wiser.

Just remember, it's a two-step process: renunciation precedes regeneration. Refrain from using words/phrases that don't add value. Regain Your use of language and know that You don't need to change anyone else. Work on *You*, and You will start to see results even with others.

You've made the decision, and have the determination to know, understand, and resolve that You won't let rust eat at You, that You will live in a world of trust. You will know with certainty that Your words matter, every single one, and that You're creating Your own narrative. Then You'll be living with exuberance and spreading the seeds of joy, happiness, peace, and love!

The Takeaways

Feel the power of this phrase: Your words matter.

Feel the "sweetness" when someone calls Your name. Especially someone You care about.

Be a COW: a Chooser of Words.

SELF TALK is the most important speech You hear.

Speech is the vessel that channels blessing into the world.

Growth with Action

List three reasons that You can say "thank You" every day .

_____

_____

_____

Seek and find a word or phrase that is a "place holder."

_____

_____

_____

Choose Your "replacement" word to eliminate the "place holder" word/ phrase.

_____

_____

_____

Find a trusted friend who will signal You when/if You use the word/ phrase that You wish to reduce/eliminate. Write down who that friend is.

_____

_____

_____

Practice saying "How can I help You?" once per day for thirty-three days.

_____

_____

_____

Strategy Six: How to Be Genuinely Kind

What does kindness look like? How does it show its face?

A kind act is something You do for and with someone with the intention of showing tenderness and affection, and without the expectation or demand of anything in return.

Here's how kindness played out for two people in a most unusual way. One was from the Middle East, the other from Mexico. The one from Mexico needed a ride. He was standing on the side of the road on a hot, dusty, Texas day in the summer. The Middle Eastern fellow stopped and offered him a ride. They both spoke in broken English as they marveled that they were about to attend the same university but in different departments and on different campuses. While the driver was supposed to be somewhere else, he made the effort to extend himself and brought this fellow on a tour of the campus and to his destination. They exchanged names, shook hands, and waved goodbye.

Years later, the Middle Eastern fellow became a successful businessman in the U.S. He learned that his mother was quite sick and needed medical attention which she couldn't get it in her home country. It was a country with no diplomatic ties to the U.S. The man wanted to get his mother to the U.S., yet there seemed to be no way. He went through as many channels as he could. He seemed to have run through them all. At his wits' end, he made a call to Washington D.C. The person who answered the call listened to the story and asked for the fellow's number. He promised to call back within forty-eight hours.

This man in Washington D.C. spent the next forty-eight hours tirelessly speaking to everyone who would listen, trying everything he could to get a mother to a safe medical facility in the U.S. When it seemed as if nothing would happen, the man made one last call. It was a homerun. He was told it could happen if they could get the woman on a flight to Vienna.

The gentleman in Washington made the call back to the Middle Eastern gentleman, as promised. The arrangements for the Vienna flight were made. With relief and in tears, the Middle Eastern fellow thanked this unknown person in Washington D.C. It was then that the fellow in Washington said, "I've been wanting to repay You for so many years."

The Middle Eastern fellow said, "But You don't know me."

"Oh yes I do," the fellow in Washington replied. "Remember when You gave me a ride in Texas? It was a very hot day and what You didn't know is that I didn't have money just then for bus fare. When You brought me on a tour of the campus and gave me lunch, I felt new life surge through me."

The mother came to the States, got treatment, saw generations of her family, and had the rest of her years in the comfort of a medical system that could care for her. But more than that, she was the embodiment of Kindness. Kindness in deed: **K**eep **I**nspiriting **N**oble **D**eeds.

Kindness and Wholeness

Being kind is a fundamental building block in the JOY of Living. A crucial feature of kindness is how it connects the heart and the mind in harmony. This will happen as Your thoughts, words, and deeds work together in concert.

We learn to be kind by hearing, listening, understanding, and then practicing. We listen for opportunities to be loving and kind knowing that this energy is the very substance that maintains all life. We are working our way to a deep understanding and practice of kindness and greater wisdom. What we pay attention to expands our minds and consciousness.

Being Kind Without Being Exploited

As we expand in our willingness to be kind, we find that there are times when our kindness can be taken advantage of. There are those who seek to use the kindness that we extend to them as a means for selfish ends. They can be alcoholics, drug addicts, compulsive overeaters, debtors, the list goes on. Somewhere in their development, they have faced such horrific circumstances that they are constantly looking for happiness anywhere but inside themselves. They are lost.

So, sometimes when we offer them a kindness, it looks to them like a weakness and they seek to exploit it. They have turned something that was a good act by us into a means for their own narrow ends.

The good news is that we don't have to repay selfishness with unkindness. Instead, we can be an example to those who can't find kindness inside themselves. This actually enables us to practice being a light where there is so little light. We don't have to be used by others, but we can love them from the distance that they have themselves created.

Here is where it gets really important. EVERYONE, that's with capitals, *everyone* You meet is fighting a battle You know nothing about. Be kind, always. As the Dalai Lama says, with that unique twinkle in his eyes, "Be kind whenever possible—and it's always possible."

One of the great hopes for those lost in addiction and seeking a path forward is the series of steps in Alcoholics Anonymous. There are twelve steps, but the first one brings a person 50% of the way to success. This first step states, "We admit we are powerless over alcohol (or any other addictive destructive behavior) and that our lives have become unmanageable."

Taking this first step and admitting You have a (drinking) problem can be difficult and scary, but it is the foundation of all positive change.

When people are addicted, they have to face the fact that they are being unkind to the person/people closest to themselves. And that is: they are being unkind to their very own self.

By overcoming stubbornness, the need for negativity, and joylessness, people can learn to live a life of kindness. By becoming an example of courage and determination and overcoming the burden of anger and addiction, kindness becomes an essential ingredient of success. And the result is living in JOY, daily.

I know this. Firsthand.

My paralysis was accompanied by almost constant pain and I was given medication to reduce and manage it. Over the course of many months, the pain receded but the mental desire/"need" for the medication didn't. I was hooked. At first, my addiction appeared as a not-so-subtle means of manipulating the system meant to keep me at ease, but in time the doctors recognized that there was no real "need" other than my desire.

Weeks of agonizing withdrawal followed when the orders were given not to administer the painkillers. The result was another drug taking over. Since I wasn't moving, I never became physically exhausted, so sleep was elusive at best. Thus, a sleep medication became my "best friend." Suffice it to say, it took almost eleven years of concerted effort to stop using drugs. The agony of withdrawal was sweat-inducing and harsh. However, the continued use of them was even harsher. Intellectually I knew all this. It was the mental dependence wherein the battle lay. Yes, I know all about addiction and its lure and control.

Those who do battle and succeed are to be respected, in my estimation.

Nobility Obliges

Here is an example of being kind, always. As mentioned earlier, due to a series of events, I became quadriplegic in 2004. My wife of twenty-seven years was left with an impossible burden. She had to maintain the family and she was without my income. Friends and acquaintances recognized our need and came to our aid. Someone I knew, but not even that well, saw the need for relief and organized a network of people in our community and business and raised more than $50,000 dollars. There was no "GoFundMe" back then!

But there was kindness, the soil of the caring heart. Such kindness allowed our family to have breathing room. It is an experience like that which makes the world soft for the weak and noble for the strong.

When we were weak, our friends and acquaintances chose the route of nobility.

So, the noble protect the weak and the weak experience a softness that shelters them.

Personifying Kindness

When You hear the word "kind," who comes to mind? Your own mother? Your father? I hope so. I hope that You did not have an abusive childhood. If You did, I am deeply sorry, but for the moment let's focus on someone You found to be kind. A teacher? Coach? Friend? A stranger? Maybe Mother Teresa?

Someone will come to mind when You focus. And that moment of kindness lasts. Now imagine being that doer of kindness.

We can think back on the kindnesses of our lives, times when someone gave us a kind word. A smile. A knowing nod of recognition for good. It may have put us back on our feet after a mishap or gave us courage or reframed the way we thought of things. A kind word can benefit someone more than money because it changes their way of thinking. The words that You say stay around, falling gently upon the rich soil of a beautiful soul.

Think of investing in Your character like investing in stocks, with one powerful difference: You can't lose! Think of Amazon when it was available at $15/share; now it's over $3,000/share and has split several times. Isn't that a *wow*?

But how much more valuable and long-lasting the investment in Your own character, especially in the area of being kind?

Practical Steps Towards Kindness

One way to make this investment is by creating and maintaining Your "thinking journal." In this powerful purposeful journal, list two acts of kindness that You did for someone else. Today. And every day going forward. Keep this journal for the next 183 days.

For this practice, You'll need to have no days with a zero. If You miss a day, just begin again, until You hit 183 days straight.

Think of this as a sequential process, not as a series of unrelated events. Think of this exercise as building wealth using the "8th wonder of the world" (per Warren Buffet): compound interest. Instead of going into Your bank account, this goes into building a joyful, prosperous, and meaningful life.

Note: it is best to do this in writing and with paper as it penetrates and connects Your thoughts and deeds. This is more effective than using a computer or Your phone.

Here's one more practical tool for creating a sense of kindness. It's a series of affirmations based on "I am." Some examples are: "I am a giver," "I am generous," "I am a helper," "I am of benefit for me and others." If needed, include "I am sober."

Affirmations done in the morning and again in the evening (most importantly in the evening before sleep to prepare the subconscious) will enable You to move Yourself forward to the person You want to become.

Kindness Echoes Down Through the Years

Here's a story of how kindness can be worth millions! When I was in my early thirties, I met an older couple who were delightful, wondrous, and successful in every way. They invited me to go with them and others on Sunday mornings to visit senior people living in nursing homes. We were there to tell stories, sing, and generally give the residents some happy hours. You could see the joy in their faces, and how they would emerge from their solitude and recognize the liveliness that we were sharing with them. I still feel it these decades later. Kindness leaves its mark.

Here's how that kindness from the past paid itself back in the present. After my experience giving service at the senior living center, I could not imagine myself living in a place like that. Despite all the joy we could bring, it could not overcome the overwhelming sadness of the place. I wanted to avoid having my wife and I living like that in our final years. One of the women in our group was in the insurance business and talked to us about a long-term care insurance plan that would enable us to be in our home in our last years. Excellent. We bought. Fifteen years later, I became paralyzed and the long-term care policy took effect. I have help twelve hours/day, seven days/week. The policy is for the life of the patient. Thus far it has paid out over One Million Dollars. A benefit of kindness that has played out over the years.

A kindness can be momentary, last an hour, an afternoon, or decades; it doesn't really matter. Just feel the joy those elderly, often infirm, people had in the short time we were there. Actions like these make a difference in people's lives and even impact generations. I recall vividly friends in the diamond business who were shaking hands on deals oftentimes worth millions of dollars based on the fact that both parties had grandparents who had done business together. It's things like this that give us greater awareness of the power, reach, and impact of kindness in the world.

You can see that there are so many kindnesses that we can share with each other. Therefore, it makes sense to keep track of them so that we remember how we can live in this fundamental aspect of joy.

The Takeaways

Everyone You meet is fighting a battle You know nothing about—be kind. Always.

KIND=Keep Inspiring Noble Deeds.

Every act of kindness done by You or for You is a ray of sunshine and hope.

No one knows the true value of a kindness.

As the Dalai Lama says: be kind whenever possible. And it's always possible.

Growth with Action

Name three acts of kindness that You plan to do today.

_____

_____

_____

_____

Journal the kindnesses that You do daily as You build Your muscle.

_____

_____

_____

_____

Perform three conscious acts of kindness this week. Do them conscientiously. Record them.

_____

_____

_____

_____

Consider sharing Your new insights into being KIND with one, maximum two, friends/family. Write down the name/s of those You will share with.

_____

_____

_____

_____

Strategy Seven: Get Out of Your Comfort Zone

She was a most radiant being. Sparkling green eyes and long flowing hair around a lovely, symmetrical face with a slight smile on it. I raised my hand and waved her over to sit next to me. What happened next shocked me.

She got up, moved across the crowded room, and sat down. We had never met before. But for the next six months it was an intense romance of the kind that only nineteen-year-olds can have.

In walking over to me, Susan got out of her comfort zone. Way out. And she told me she had no idea why she would ever get up and walk across a crowded room to sit with a stranger. But she did. And I had no idea what prompted me to wave my hand, beckoning her. Who does such a thing? But I did.

And we both learned that being UN-comfortable can lead to remarkable situations.

It's as my uncle Eddie had said to me so many times: *risk being happy*.

"Well that's pretty easy for a nineteen-year-old," You might say.

Okay, but it didn't feel that way. Uncomfortable is uncomfortable, whether You've lived twenty-nine years or thirty-nine years. Or forty-nine, fifty-nine, or sixty-nine! How about ninety-nine? Why limit it?

A Centenarian Gets UN-Comfortable

"Hi Barry. Sing me a song."

That's how Aida greets me. She's 108 (!) now and we've shared a lane at the local aquatic center (fancy term for the pool) for over twelve years, since I first started swimming.

Aida was brought to the aquatic center by her caretaker to walk *in* the water. It's the best exercise for her: very gentle on the body and no worry about slipping and falling because she holds on to the lane line. Well, at the age of ninety-five she was still "with it" mentally and enjoyed seeing me go from the wheelchair to the special lift that puts You into the water and brings You back up. She uses it as well.

We got to speaking. She said, "I love Your attitude. I'm ninety-five, but just not that happy. Can You help me?"

Hello: she's ninety-five and willing to *learn*! So, we began slowly using some of the techniques from the 11 Strategies. (See Aida and Barry with the 11 Strategies book at: barryshore.com/aida.)

And which do You think resonates the most with Aida? You got it. Get UN-comfortable. She says it helps her stay sharp and "thinking."

Yes, this really is the strategy that resonates most with my wise, centenarian friend. "Move out of Your comfort zone," says Aida. Whatever Your chronological age. This really means to become UN-comfortable. I'm not suggesting putting a pebble in Your shoe or wearing a hair shirt. I'm suggesting something deeper.

Now You might ask, "Why should I be uncomfortable? After all, isn't it important to be warm at night, and to have enough food and water, to be well-clothed and cared-for?" Yes. But we're talking about the ability to move out of the comfort zone of Your *mind*. Metaphorically, we clothe ourselves with different garments. We often protect our emotional life with lies, misdirection, and willful ignorance. These things become like a shell, instead of being loose-fitting and soft. Our fearful insistence on being comfortable actually becomes like body armor.

Comfort is an insatiable monster. It's where dreams go to die.

Responding to Discomfort

"She said this horrible thing." "I actually saw this injustice." "He/she irritates me."

These feelings seem negative, but they are great because You have Your positive, powerful antidote at the ready: Your thinking journal. Instead of ignoring these negative feelings and clothing Your mind with ignorance, face these feelings. In Your journal, at least once a week—preferably twice—write down the action, or idea, or whatever else You recognize that causes You DIS-comfort. Once You begin recognizing these DIS-comforting items/ideas/thoughts, You're going to be able to deal with them.

Remember that the three principles that underlie everything are always true:

> Your life has a purpose; Go MAD; and unlock the power
> and secrets of everyday words and terms.

You are learning to respond differently as You continue to absorb these ideas and practical practices. Use them as an exercise machine, and as You grow with them, You will build Your consciousness because You become more aware of the positivity in Your everyday world.

Obviously, You can't control the world, but You *can* control your response to it.

Treasures of the Deep

The natural world also gives us an example of how discomfort can yield precious gifts. If You take an oyster and place a small irritant inside it and then replace the oyster back into its sea bed, the oyster covers the irritant. This buildup is called nacre and creates the luster on what becomes a pearl.

Think of Your own life this way. As You move into the uncomfortable, You're building your own pearl. Events in Your life will grow around You and form something beautiful and unique. Sometimes it just takes us moving out of our comfort zone to create our own lustrous jewel.

So, in an interesting way, You can begin to thank those people who annoy You—and by so doing You're changing Your thought power from annoyance to gratitude. Instead of feeling inconvenienced or uncomfortable, You can actually learn to say, "I'm grateful for _____," and You will begin to experience a deep peace. It's stronger, longer lasting, and more beautiful than the discomfort that You felt.

I first began getting UN-comfortable when, as a teenager, an older friend recommended I learn to brush my teeth using my non-dominant hand. What? Why? He said: trust me. You'll thank me eventually. Well I did it for years and it never felt right but it did teach me the important lesson: get UN-comfortable and get conscious. And now the science shows that brushing Your teeth with Your non-dominant hand improves brain function and encourages new neural pathways. Using the non-dominant hand activates both hemispheres of Your brain.

Discomfort is what makes Your mind come alive.

A Habit of Gratitude

Here is a most powerful, life-enhancing exercise that You can do for the rest of Your life. Yes, every day from now forward. By using these (IMHO) two most important words in the English language consciously and conscientiously three times per day, You will Make A Difference in Your life and in the lives of everyone around You.

And these words are:

Thank You.

Thank You. Thank You.

THANK stands for **T**o **H**armonize **A**nd **N**etwork **K**indness. As we noted before, the Dalai Lama advises: be kind whenever possible...and it's always possible!

You go to the coffee shop and order Your fancy latte for $5.50 and someone brings it to You: Thank You.

You're walking out of the coffee shop and it's raining outside, and someone holds the door open for You: Thank You.

You're walking out of the coffee shop and it's raining outside, and someone slams the door on You: Thank You.

You're in traffic and late for an appointment and someone cuts You off: Thank You.

You get up in the middle of the night and You stub Your toe and it hurts: Thank You.

To **H**armonize **A**nd **N**etwork **K**indness.

That's Your world when You consciously enter get UN-comfortable.

You'll soar.

Three Practices for Gratitude in Discomfort

Here are three simple, easy practices that will encourage You to see the world in gratitude while You step out of Your comfort zone.

The first. When You leave home and walk a few paces in whatever direction You normally would go, stop and turn and walk the other way. Change the route at least once a day for a week. You will have challenged and overcome Your comfort zone. This will help You to shatter any self-imposed limit.

The second practice is to make a change in the route You take to get to your destination/work. Yes, it may take an extra five to ten minutes, but You will be consciously claiming Your birthright: You make the decisions. We all get habituated to certain situations. No matter the habit, adjust it. And feel the power of mastery.

The third one is actually one of the hardest ones. Whatever time You get up daily, alter that by moving the time back five minutes. The reason here is that controlling Your time is controlling the most powerful and potent force at Your command. Your sleep time is so important that when You make the decision to move Your awakening time back, You will eventually adjust Your going-to-bed time. Make a note in Your thinking journal about how You feel regarding this most vital exercise. It's not easy. It is highly rewarding. Feel free to contact me about Your progress.

Working with these three exercises will enable You to alter Your relationship to time and space. By changing Your relationship to Your traditional rising time, You will transcend time. By adjusting Your direction and Your daily route, You will transcend space. With all of these together, You will become acutely aware that everything in Your world is under Your command.

The ability to transcend time and space in the awareness that everything is, in its essence, Divinity is a principle cause for JOY.

The Takeaways

Comfort is a hungry monster.

Comfort is where dreams go to die.

Shift matters. Even a small shift out of Your comfort zone can produce major results.

Mind is the Master. You decide Your movements.

Gratitude is that emotion with the longest shelf life.

Growth with Action

Special ideas for Your reclaimed five Minutes:

Become a JOY Generator: 55 seconds once per day
(https://www.barryshore.com/joygenerator).

Be Calm & Aware: 94 seconds twice per day
(https://www.barryshore.com/94seconds).

What are three actions You can take to leverage Your insights about being UN-comfortable ?

_____

_____

_____

_____

Put these into Your practice journal.

Strategy Eight: No More Perfectionism!

Maybe it was the minty Life Saver smell that always intrigued me. Or the glassy eyes. Or just a bit of wobbly walk. Mr. Campbell was certainly a capable math teacher and my tutor in helping me understand "the calculus," as he called it. (It didn't stick—I never gained a good grasp of higher math.) And people said later that he did drink—regularly. But I am most appreciative of something he made me aware of when I tried to excuse my not having prepared my assignments: "Son, there are many reasons for failure; but no excuse."

Spot on. Thank You, Mr. Campbell. It did take many more years to integrate this insight into my core being and actions. Nevertheless, it was helpful in the interim as I observed others and myself. Until I finally realized: *Aha.* Truth. And acted accordingly. To my great benefit financially, mentally, and spiritually.

How the Great Man Became Great

"Do what you can, with what you have, where you are."

—*Theodore Roosevelt.*

One of America's larger-than-life heroes was a man who lived as he thought.

Roosevelt was a sickly youth. Physically, it was very difficult for him to do many things, so he used his mind to train his body. But Roosevelt's goal was not to become just physically fit. His goal was to do his best and become as strong and good as he could by using his maximum effort. As a result, he became a great warrior, a great president, a great father, a great husband, a great statesman, and a winner of the Nobel Peace Prize. He lived what he called a "bully life" full of "vim and vigor." All this was because he knew the importance of always doing his best and training his mind for success. There was good reason that his likeness was carved into Mount Rushmore.

In 1910, he delivered one of the most inspirational, impassioned, and often-quoted speeches in American history:

> *It is not the critic who counts; not the man who points out how the strong man stumbles, or where the doer of deeds could have done them better. The credit belongs to the man who is actually in the arena, whose face is marred by dust and sweat and blood; who strives valiantly; who errs, who comes short again and again, because there is no effort without error and shortcoming; but who does actually strive to do the deeds; who knows great enthusiasms, the great devotions; who spends himself in a worthy cause; who at the best knows in the end the triumph of high achievement, and who at the worst, if he fails, at least fails while daring greatly, so that his place shall never be with those cold and timid souls who neither know victory nor defeat.*

What Roosevelt's example teaches us is that You can work on Yourself by carefully examining who You are. We do spend our entire lives with our "self" and the ability to harmonize and be at peace with one's self is the truest level of success.

Changing Your Story, Changing Your Brain

The narrative we tell ourselves is the way we transform our existence. In reality, each of us is a STAR: **S**unshine **T**ransformed **A**nd **R**eformatted. There are no small parts in the great drama of life; only small players. Every person can succeed at something. And every person can GO Make A Difference.

These universal truths are at the core of the 11 Strategies. With the mindset of always doing Your best, You can reclaim Your inheritance. Our brains are the most complex mechanisms in the universe, with over one-hundred billion cells and one thousand trillion synapses connecting them. (Yes, please read those numbers again...they *are* astounding.) And these cells and synapses exist for more than just deciding what kind of latte You want this morning.

In his captivating book, *The Brain's Way of Healing: Remarkable Discoveries and Recoveries from the Frontiers of Neuroplasticity*, Dr. Norman Doidge makes the case—actually, cases—for how and why the brain can "find" new pathways despite debilitating and crippling disease.

As a part of the Infinite, You have the power to create seemingly impossible feats. CREATE is a wondrous acronym that stands for **C**ausing **R**ethinking **E**nabling **A**ll **T**o **E**xcel. By rethinking the possible— by making *impossible* into I'm *possible*—we give permission for ourselves to succeed. Indeed, for all to excel.

The Perpetual Importance of Words

We can spin almost any word in the positive direction. For example, here's an acronym for BRAIN: **B**eneficial **R**ejuvenating **A**ctivity **I**ncreasing **N**urturing. It's a mouthful, but useful when You want to get a positive spin on a vital part of Your body. As You use this way of thinking about the brain, You're going to discover that adversity, risk, and daring will become something that can nurture You as You. The five words of this acronym will take on a new meaning if You remember that they are there to encourage You to *always* do Your best.

Using words for their positive effect is like using jiujitsu. We can take words that start out in a negative way and turn them on their head, giving them a positive spin. We can redirect the flow of the words we use by thinking of them in their most positive light. We can think of FLOW as **F**ocus **L**ife **O**n **W**onder. As we do this, we hone our minds to become observers of the positive, of the wonder in life. And indeed, it is a wonder!

Resetting any word or term can give it unexpected meaning. For example, F.U.! When we add one simple letter to it, the whole thing takes on a new meaning. That simple letter is "N." We have made a joyful word from an expression that is not really joyful or helpful at all.

In my work with individuals and companies, I use the "four-letter F-word" to shock people. Mr. Shore is using the F.U. word? Then I say: "F.U., everybody! But remember to *add* immediately, 'N.N.'"

Invariably people say, "But Mr. Shore, fun is spelled with only three letters."

And I respond, "Not in our world. In the world of the positive, purposeful, powerful, and pleasant, it's F.U.N.N.! Which is *fu...nn*!" Yes, tell Your friends and family "F.U." but remember to add "N.N." So, "W.T.F." now becomes "What the Funn!" It becomes the pink elephant in the room. Unforgettable. You'll always remember it.

Giving It Your Best

Your best at this moment may not be Your best in the future, but by remembering to nurture Yourself, You can continue to give Your best effort *now*.

Michelangelo was a prime example of CREATE. He rethought the way we paint, and by doing so painted the Sistine Chapel while lying on his back on a scaffold that he had built. He rethought painting by painting upside down.. His positive attitude of *rethinking* and doing his best enabled him to carve perhaps the most famous statue of all time: the statue of David, the shepherd who slew the mighty Goliath. Michelangelo looked at a discarded piece of marble and formed the most admired work of art in the world. When asked how he did so, he is said to have answered, "I looked and carved away anything that was not David." That was how dramatically his rethinking brought forth "life." He did his best and the result astounds millions.

You may say that You're not that talented. But in Your own way You are. You are continually creating the image of who and what You are from the inside out. You are a "Michelangelo" because You take the world You see and rethink it as Your own and, in being Yourself, You bring a unique being that makes a difference in the world. And I write this without exaggeration or hyperbole.

The greatest danger for most of us is not that our aim is too high, and that we don't reach it. It's that our aim is too low, and we do reach it!

Here's an example from the film world. Today a cult classic, "Rudy" was released in 1993. This is the true story of a kid with limited mental and physical capacity who manages to go to Notre Dame, a college with a powerhouse football team. Somehow, he manages to get a place on the third-string practice team. In that position, it was expected he would never play in a real game, but at every practice he gave it his all. Once, while scrimmaging, Rudy tackled the first-string quarterback.

The quarterback complained to the coach, "Hey Coach...this kid's a pain. He's playing like it's the Super Bowl!"

The coach replied, "That's exactly the point. Every play is important. And when you learn the lesson, that there are many reasons for failure but no excuse, you might fulfill your potential." Rudy made every play important. You can't succeed by going through the motions. Give Your best at all times...and You can't Fail!

In his final year, Rudy got to play in a regulation game. Everyone at the school, and in the crowd of thousands, knew his story. So, in the final game of the season, with a cheering crowd hailing him, Rudy went in for the final play of the season. And he sacked the opposing quarterback!

He was treated like the hero that he was. He was carried off the field by the crowd and his teammates, the only player in Notre Dame's history to ever have been so honored. He triumphed because he was an amazing example of *always do Your best*. He was not special or uniquely talented, he was just like the rest of us. So, continually give it Your all. Rudy did.

Your Best Will Change the World Around You

In Your thinking journal, mark down the times when You didn't think You could do something, but You gave it Your best anyway. This is how You become successful. It's often the mistakes that promote our fullest growth. Our success sometimes comes as much from our failures as our triumphs. It comes from the ability to get up again and again with undiminished enthusiasm. Tiny shifts can ripple outward to become a triumph.

We can give the world miracles by becoming like Michelangelo, who used a discarded piece of marble to create a statue of stunning and lasting beauty. Yet, You don't have to be one of the most talented human beings in the history of the world. You have a gift as unique as the one he had. You have the gift of being Yourself. You can chip away at those parts of Yourself that You don't want and You can transform Yourself into the person that You *do* imagine!

You can recast the negativity that You may see and hear around You. You can give positivity to the store clerk who is tired, angry, and at the end of their rope. You can uplift someone on the phone, even someone's who's cold calling You. Just say, "You have a tough job and I want to wish You well." When You do Your best to help another person, You're being Your best. It's a tall order, and with some practice and the help of these strategies, You can do this. Learn that HOPE stands for **H**elping **O**thers **P**rogress **E**veryday. The time You have invested and will invest, to bring into Your mind the concepts, practices, tips, and tools in this book, will enable You to succeed and to GO MAD.

The Takeaways

Remember Mr. Campbell: There are many reasons for failure but no excuses.

Remember the example of Theodore Roosevelt: by training his mind, he achieved seemingly impossible things.

By shifting Your narrative, You can CREATE like Michelangelo.

Remember always that You are a beautiful, bountiful, beloved, immortal being who is good-looking. You're good-looking because You're always looking for and finding the good. You are what You seek.

Be a HOPE dispenser.

Growth with Action

Mark down three times when You didn't think You could do something...
but gave it Your best anyway .

_____

_____

_____

_____

Write down how You felt when You did Your best and kept pushing
forward.

_____

_____

_____

_____

Tell Yourself the story of how You persevered and did Your best, as if
You're a grandparent relating it to Your grandchild.

_____

_____

_____

_____

Try something new that You are now awkward at...and resolve to do Your
best to become proficient. Set a date to accomplish Your first level of
proficiency.

_____

_____

_____

_____

Strategy Nine: The Art and Science of Friendship

The cry came up out of my heart: "Oh Ginger! Help!"

And help he did. For the next few months, Steven, aka Ginger, worked tirelessly to secure all the possible benefits from our insurance companies (yes plural) to make sure we kept our home, had our medical expenses paid, and received the care necessary. After all I was now completely paralyzed, and my wife was under enormous pressure and stress. Without a dear trusted friend, much of what was needed may not have been secured.

Steven is a highly skilled, successful attorney and litigator who understands the labyrinthine ways of dealing with complex medical issues. And more importantly, he's been my best friend since my earliest memory. In our time of need, he answered my cry for help. And he never asked for a dime.

Imagine You're friends with someone since the age of two days old. That's actually how long Steven and I have known each other. My second day in the world was when my mother and I came home from the hospital and she introduced me to Steven, he of the flaming red hair (hence his nickname, "Ginger").

Our mothers were best friends. Our parents lived in the same apartment building in Boston. Steven was born twenty-two days before me. Our mothers were like sisters and we called each other's parents "aunt" and "uncle" and considered ourselves cousins. That was seventy-plus years ago and, aside from very different politics, we are still close and—most importantly—trust each other. Which of course is the essence of this particular strategy.

Having a few good friends is foundational to a JOY-filled life.

But what is a friend? And how can You be a friend?

We'll look at the answers in this chapter.

Friends of Legend

"Friends helps us deal with stress, make better lifestyle choices that keep us strong, and allow us to rebound from health issues and disease more quickly."

—Liveabout.com

Have You ever heard of Damon and Pythias? Get ready for an amazing story.

Damon and Pythias lived under King Dionysius in Syracuse, Greece, over two thousand years ago. The king was ruthless, angry, and a harsh ruler. Therefore, he was a lonely man. Untrusting, and untrustworthy, all his power could not buy him a friend.

Damon and Pythias, on the other hand, were true and devoted friends. Both were students of the school of Pythagoras, the famous Greek mathematician who taught that theorems and proofs were part of a larger ethical program based on timeless truth. Pythias believed it was correct to speak out about the abuses of Dionysius. When Dionysius heard about his public speeches, he had Pythias brought before him. Pythias's close friend Damon came along.

The King, furious at the truth-telling Pythias, had his court condemn him to die. Pythias accepted the sentence with equanimity but asked the ruler for one final request. That request was to be allowed to return to his hometown and set his affairs in order.

Dionysius laughed. "If I give You permission, what guarantee do I have that You will return? Why would You come back to face Your own death?"

At that point Damon stepped forward. "I will take his place and stand surety."

"If he does not come back, You will die in his place."

Damon accepted.

The date and time were set for the execution.

On the day of the execution, Pythias had not returned.

"You see, Your friend has not returned." The ruler felt relieved that his estimation of human nature had proved true.

Damon said merely, "He will return. He is a man of his word."

The hours passed and still no Pythias.

Damon was brought to the executioner's block.

At that moment, Pythias burst in. Exhausted, muddied, and bloodied, he said, "I am sorry I'm late. My ship was wrecked in a storm, and bandits attacked me on the road and took my horse, but a good man lent me his. I am here to accept my sentence."

Astounded at the friendship between the two men, and the complete loyalty, reliability, and willingness to sacrifice they displayed, Dionysius was moved. He had never witnessed, nor did he think it possible, to have such a friend.

Astounded, Dionysius walked to the men and put his hands out in greeting. He released both men and commuted the sentence.

He said, "You have taught me what true friendship looks like. You have given me the greatest gift. I now know what a friend is. You are free to go."

Talk about "got Your back." What an example!

Making Modern Friendship Meaningful

The word *friend* is a powerful and deeply meaningful word. Friendship is foundational to the 11 Strategies for Living in JOY because it marks the difference between conscious humanity and unconscious living. We all have friends. But in the twenty-first century, the meaning of the word is so watered down that we use the term loosely to include any kind of contact—even just electronic.

Compare the friendship of Damon and Pythias to that of Your "Facebook friends," or those of other social media platforms. Often these are "friends" we've never met and we have had very little or no personal interaction with them. Often, we don't even have many shared values.

The word *friend* has a deeper meaning. Through thousands of years of recorded history, it has been a positive, powerful, and important term. *Friend* has played a vital role in every language and culture. In English we say, "A friend in need is a friend indeed." The deed is really the key. You saw that in the actions of Damon and Pythias.

Let's have some fun and examine the word *friend*. If You remove the letter "R" from *friend*, You are left with *fiend*. A fiend is someone unpleasant and to be avoided. The difference between the two words is the letter "R." To me, "R" stands for *reliable*. That is an essential part of what a friend is. At the end of the word is a "D," which stands for *dependable*. Again, think of the example of Damon and Pythias.

I was blessed growing up. I had a friend whose father taught us a key lesson about friendship when we were in our early teens. My friend's father said, "Guys, friends are great; best thing in the world next to wife and family. If You can count Your friends on Your thumbs, You're doing well in life." He paused and added, "I hope that it happens for both of You."

Fast forward decades later. It still reverberates. Friendship, both being one and having one, have been crucial to my success in life. "Two thumbs." You're doing well with two true friends. All these years later, that still rings true for me.

"A friend in need is a friend indeed." A friend has two aspects. You must be a good friend to have one. And when You are dependable and reliable, You will attract people and create bonds built on these cornerstones. When Your words and deeds convey trust, You will be able to acquire a friend.

Helping One Another

As iron sharpens iron, so a person sharpens his friend."

—*Proverbs 27:17*

Trust is the key to understanding the human condition. One way to view TRUST is: **T**otal **R**eliance **U**pon **S**omething **T**rue.

The story of Helen Keller and Anne Sullivan is a well-known true friendship that has been dramatized in a movie and play called *The Miracle Worker*. Due to an illness, Helen lost her sight and hearing before the age of two, then struggled to find her place in the world. In 1887, a twenty-year-old Anne Sullivan, arrived at the Keller's Alabama home to become the young girl's teacher. Helen was initially highly combative with Sullivan, but one day associated water flowing over her hand with Sullivan using her fingers to spell the word "water" on her palm. This breakthrough provided a means for Helen to "see the world" and eventually communicate with others and unlock her prodigious talents and abilities.

With Sullivan's assistance, Helen was able to pursue educational opportunities in New York and Massachusetts. Sullivan remained at Helen's side, using finger spelling to convey lectures and conversations to the younger woman. Though it hurt her own eyesight, Sullivan also reviewed textbooks to deliver the information to Helen. In those days there were not enough Braille textbooks for Helen to read the coursework on her own.

In true friendship form, Helen helped Sullivan in turn. While at Radcliffe, Keller could tell her teacher's eyes were hurting due to the amount of reading she was doing. Helen later admitted that at times "when she asked if I did not want certain passages re-read, I lied and declared that I could recall them," so as to spare Sullivan further eyestrain.

Through their time together, Sullivan, who was always haunted by a horrific childhood stay in a poorhouse, knew she could depend on Helen for support. When Sullivan's health failed, and she became blind in the 1930s, Helen aided her teacher with tasks such as writing letters. And her work with Helen offered Sullivan a feeling of accomplishment. In a manuscript she called "Foolish Remarks of a Foolish Woman," Anne Sullivan wrote "Only in Helen have I kept the fire of a purpose alive. Every other dream flame has been blown out by some interfering fool."

Helen Keller impacted hundreds of millions of people worldwide. It could not have happened without the dedication and trust of her friend, Anne Sullivan.

Says the ancient proverb, "Either friendship or death."

Finding True Value

What do You value? Money more than time? Trust more than money? Being "in" more than being reliable? Your greatest values are what You attract into Your world. If You haven't yet articulated Your values, please do so now.

Please take a blank piece of paper and write down three ideals that You value most in each of the following areas: family, work, money.

Do this now. These values may change over time, but they won't change drastically. Your list may be edited, it may be honed, it may be extended, but it is crucial to look at what You consider valuable in Your life. Right now.

Because it's what You're going to attract into Your life.

Surprisingly, this is not an easy or simple exercise. It is however essential to Your success. Articulating Your values opens the pathways of this powerful, beneficial process.

Because above all, the most important friend You have is: You. When You become the best You possible, You make a difference in the world. You build bridges and create more harmony, which brings about more JOY, happiness, peace, and love.

This above all: to thine own self be true,

And it must follow, as the night the day,

Thou canst not then be false to any man.

—*Hamlet Act 1, Scene 3 (emphasis mine)*

Sage advice from a father to his son.

Shining Like a STAR

Growth needs healthy soil, the right nutrients, water, and sunshine. In other words, the right environment. Having these, You will shine like a STAR, which is **S**unshine **T**ransformed **A**nd **R**eformatted. As the noted scientist and astronomer Carl Sagan quipped, "We are all sunshine."

Here are three steps to become a STAR:

1. Find a mentor/teacher/coach that You admire and that You know has Your best interest at heart.
2. Acquire a friend.
3. Judge all people favorably.

You will recognize Your teacher because You will learn from him/her and will relate to what they have to say. And how they act. And their insight and advice will be straightforward and helpful. Don't seek sugarcoating and ego-stroking. Seek accountability.

You acquire a friend by investing Your time and energy in cultivating a relationship.

Finally, judge all people to the side of merit, until You know firsthand that they will not respond to Your kindly nature.

These three processes enable You to grow.

A Lifelong Pursuit

Friendship spans decades and transcends both time and space.

Here are three fundamental questions that we ask as we prepare for whatever life brings us:

1. How honestly do You deal with other people?
2. Do You treat Your family with love and respect?
3. Are You involved in helping others?

These are values clarification questions that can and should apply to Your friendships as well.

To deepen this and integrate it into Your life, take that paper with Your ideal values and write down who Your closest friends are and whom You depend upon. These are people who really have shown, "I have your back." These are family and friends who demonstrate their friendship by their deeds.

And now, just as importantly, write down that You are committed to be a friend in return!

Words matter. **W**ords **O**f **W**isdom (WOW) are like dew upon the grass: gentle, nourishing, enlivening. Words that come from the heart penetrate the heart, but sometimes the heart must break for us to hear the truth. It is often with friends that we hear the truth. It is part of why we are together.

Having and being a friend is a lifelong pursuit. I have been fortunate enough to share a lifetime with my dear wife, Naomi. She is the friend that I trust completely. She gives me encouragement and is not afraid to point out times when I need reshaping. Discouragement is part of life. As we share life, we need both encouragement and the truth. It's a balance. Words from a friend never upset the balance; they add stability.

In this way we build our CORE: our **C**hannel of **O**ngoing **R**ejuvenating **E**nergy. That's Your ability to be a conduit for the growth of Your friend and Yourself. It consists in being able to accept things about Yourself that You may need to alter, change, let go of, or nurture.

As the insight from the 12 Step program teaches: Please grant me the serenity to accept the things I cannot change, the ability to change the things I can, and the wisdom to know the difference.

A vital part of friendship is refraining from gossip. It's an honor and a privilege to be able to share something intimate and personal with a friend. He or she has given us a trust that is precious. For us to break that trust would wound that agreement and injure the relationship in a fundamental and perhaps unrecoverable way. Therefore, never divulge a secret and never gossip. Never.

Go forward with Your friends and be a changemaker in the world. They will thank You and You will create much good as You prosper and flourish.

The Takeaways

Friend depends upon the R and D: Reliability and Dependability.

Life depends upon the trust of a friend.

If You can count Your friends on Your thumbs,
You're doing well.

Be a friend and acquire a friend.

Never gossip.

Growth with Action

Write down Your three top values in each of these areas:

Family, Work, Money:

_____

_____

_____

_____

_____

_____

_____

Do You know a secret about Your friends/s that should never be shared?

_____

_____

_____

_____

Do You recognize why Your friend/s placed such trust in You? Write the quality/ies that You exhibit that engender trust.

_____

_____

_____

_____

Write Your answers to the three major questions of life:

1.   Do You deal honestly with people?

_____

_____

_____

_____

_____

2.   Do You treat Your family with love and respect?

_____

_____

_____

_____

3.   Are You involved in helping others?

_____

_____

_____

_____

Strategy Ten: Find Peace from Within

This is the most powerful and probably the most difficult of all the 11 Strategies. It touches the very essence of the human condition. We're built to live in society, with family, and with friends. We also align ourselves in groups for the purposes of business. We are social animals and have been wired to want recognition within our group. Another name for this kind of recognition is honor. How You deal with and handle honor is the discussion of this chapter.

A Woman of Honor

She was a quiet, shy, attractive Oriental woman with a matronly bearing, despite the fact that she was only twenty-eight years old (which I only found out months later). She was the gatekeeper for the president of the school where I taught. My very outgoing—she would later call it *loud*—demeanor was certainly not to her liking. And yet she liked me. Go figure.

Poradee (yes, that's her birth name) is the most authentic, unprepossessing (I like writing the word!) person I have met in my over seventy years on the planet. She is the model and embodiment of the strategy we'll be discussing in this chapter. How do I know? I've been married to her for over forty-four years now.

Suffice it to say that there are many stories, adventures, and remarkable incidences in any marriage of decades. Ours is compounded and multiplied by different upbringings, cultures, and traumatic events. Not the least is the incidence of my becoming paralyzed overnight and my wife (who, for over forty years now, has chosen to go by "Naomi") having to bear the weight of taking care of our family, the business, the enormous medical expenses, and the details that would overwhelm a battery of accountants and psychologists. And she did all this with a grand spirit and capability that defies my abilities to articulate.

She had no need to prove herself. She took care of everything that needed to be done without fanfare, applause, or breakdown. Except once. And that ended in a major benefit for her paralyzed husband. (More about that later.)

I know that this strategy—approaching life without the need to prove Yourself—works because I have seen it work in someone to whom it comes naturally.

I have seen it in Naomi.

And in this chapter, I will take what I have learned from her—and others—and pass it on to You.

Struggling Towards an Answer About Identity

The beauty of life emerges through struggle.

Imagine You can hear a seed growing. You can hear its struggle to find water with roots breaking through its outer shell. Then pushing up through the earth as it reaches for sunshine. It's always involved in struggle but what emerges is the miracle called *life*. So, the very essence of what we are discussing here begins with something that is part and parcel of nature, which is the human condition. It asks the great existential question of "Who are You?"

Who am I? What are my goals? What do I want to accomplish? Who do I want to be in this process? During the 1960s there was a TV show called "The Art Linkletter Show" and it was subtitled, "Kids Say the Darndest Things." One episode was particularly memorable. One of the kids was asked, "What does Your father do?"

"Oh, he's a rat."

Linkletter looked puzzled.

"Well...he tells me he's in the rat race."

My father was watching with me and said, "The interesting part of the rat race is that even when You win, You're still a rat. That's how this kid's father was thinking."

My dad continued, "Your mind is the master. There's no need to prove Yourself, except to Yourself. When You know who You are, then You don't need outside validation. You're capable of knowing when You're in a situation where You're seeking status or honor. You decide to choose the ladder of true success. Never let anyone or any group do that for You."

I really had no idea what my father was talking about for another fifteen years or so, but the kid on the show did stick with me. I didn't want to be in a rat race.

So, my dad was teaching me that the first and most important step on this ladder is awareness. Who am I? What am I doing? Why am I doing this?

These are questions that almost always come up in the course of everyone's life at some point. Seeking out the answers to them is liberating. Unfortunately, the most usual response is: *later.*

"*Later*" is the first step to "never."

We avoid giving an actual answer to these important questions because once we begin to answer, our next step is action. We become aware and act.

Sometimes what keeps us from answering are intangible things—things like worry or distraction.

But sometimes what keeps us from answering is very tangible, very practical, and very—dare I say it?—*material.*

Sometimes what keeps us from answering is money.

Where Money Meets Identity

The most common form of the question, "Who are You?" is the one You'll hear at any social function where strangers are meeting. It is, of course, "And what do You do?"

Isn't that funny? Who You are is usually defined by what You do and by how much money You earn. Dangerous waters, but they must be navigated.

Here's a vital question. Who is rich? Who is really wealthy? My very successful uncle would often tell me, "Money never made anyone rich." I always found that easy for him to say since he seemed to have so much. He did teach me that in business money is a wonderful tool but it's just a tool. If You become subject to it, then You are its slave.

His favorite aphorism was: *Money is a horrible taskmaster but a fabulous servant.*

Powerful, prophetic, and useful words for a budding entrepreneur.

But is it true? Is this what the world reflects? In my humble opinion, the answer was, *no.*

At least, that's what I thought until I met and did business with some of the most celebrated/famous people in Hollywood.

Then I saw that, with a rare exception here and there, my rich uncle's words were true.

And that's why this particular strategy is so important. It may be the cornerstone of the entire edifice. Unless and until You can approach this most fundamental question and answer convincingly for Yourself, it's difficult to live a truly success-filled life.

Here's something that I sang with my son and other kids while driving the carpool. "If You have Your eyes and Your teeth and Your hands and Your feet, You are a very rich person." We'd go through it a number of times so that the kids could sing the refrain and I would add each child's name into the song. They enjoyed it. Most days.

I enjoyed it too because it challenged me to think about the benefits of eyes and teeth and hands and feet. Did I ever imagine that I would need this song when I didn't have use of most of my limbs?

No, of course not.

Songs like this are the very essence of being happy or satisfied with what You have. This is the fundamental ingredient in recognizing that there's no need to prove Yourself. When You're happy with Your lot, You're rich! Let's review this. I'm not advising You to say, "Okay, I'm satisfied with what I/we have." I'm writing that You should be happy with whatever You have.

Hey come on now. You want me to be a saint?

Comparison is the death of true self-contentment.

—*John Powell*

No. Be human. Be real. Is there a contradiction in being happy with life and wanting to improve Your situation? No. The issue here is knowing, deep inside, that there's no need to prove Yourself to anyone except Yourself. The trappings of outward success are just that: *traps.*

Recent studies show that sixty-eight percent (68%!) of Americans are mildly depressed and/or dissatisfied with their lives regardless of their social status or job. How is this possible? America is the most prosperous, opportunity-oriented country in the history of the world. But it's because people haven't learned or internalized what You're learning. *There is no need to prove Yourself.*

If You've got Your eyes and Your teeth, Your hands and Your feet, You are a very rich person. Teeth. We tend to be obsessed these days with whitening our teeth. Now, I really enjoy my teeth. I haven't had a cavity in decades. I take good care of them. Teeth are fantastic. But if You don't have them, and a lot of people don't and have to get dentures, it makes a big difference. Hands. When You see a video of me, You'll notice my hands are crooked and the fingers don't close. Do I have arthritis? No. I woke up one morning hale, hearty, and healthy and able to leap tall buildings in a single bound. Then, that evening, I was in the hospital paralyzed from my neck down, from a rare neurological disease. So, the fact that I can even move my hands is great. I still can't pick up certain things and I can't close my fingers, but I have functional hands.

I have legs and feet. I still can't move my feet up and down or wiggle my toes, but I can use them to be ambulatory with the help of a walking device. I can't climb up a stair by myself or walk up a curb, and I need help twelve hours/day, seven days/week. But I am happy with what I have. There is no need to prove myself.

OWN it NOW

Here is an exercise to help You gauge how happy You are with what You have. In Your journal, write down—or right here on this very page!—that You are *committed* to saying "Thank You," consciously and conscientiously, three times a day. Why? Because THANK stands for: To Harmonize And Network Kindness.

You are unique. You know the old saw: no two people with the same fingerprints. Voice prints. Ever. In the history of the world. So, let's focus on what You *can* do in the here and now to be the *full* You.

Write it down now because there's power in NOW. NOW stands for **N**o **O**ther **W**ay. When You do it now, You own it. OWN is the acronym for **O**nly **W**ith **N**ow. Then when You've done that, You've won. WON is **W**ith **O**nly **N**ow. So, it's all about the now, the ability to act.

Later is the first step to never.

By committing to saying Thank You three times per day, every day for the rest of Your life (*yes*, the rest of Your life!), You are recognizing that You are a conduit of goodness. The point of this simple yet powerful exercise is to make You aware that You possess a wealth, a vast abundance of goodness that You can dispense. Givers gain. That is the essence of living in JOY, daily. Being a giver is an aspect of wealth. By knowing that You are a very rich/wealthy person, You can continue to build Your giving muscle and become the best You possible.

Is this not a wonder-filled reason to live? There's no need to prove Yourself to anyone other than Your true self. And Your very self is a giver.

Awareness Leads to Action

The proper function of man is to live, not to exist. I shall not waste my days in trying to prolong them. I shall use my time more wisely.

—Jack London, *American author*

Recall that the first step in the ladder for success is awareness. The next step is action. Funny, but we do live in a world of seeming paradox: at one and the same time there is freedom in discipline and there is bondage in license. Your free decision to discipline Yourself makes the difference. And note that the word discipline has within it, *disciple*. The freedom of discipline comes when You're in the flow and You're making things happen; then You really do have the freedom to choose to respond and not just to react.

To respond consciously in any situation enables You to channel Your energies.. Structure doesn't impinge; it liberates. The greatest example of this in terms of power is to note the difference between a flashlight and a laser beam. A flashlight shines diffused light, but when You concentrate that same light and stimulate and amplify the light, it can cut through steel. That's a laser beam; that's disciplined channeling. It doesn't impinge; it liberates.

Caring for Others Without Caring About Their Opinions

You don't have to prove Yourself to anybody else. We may know intellectually that we shouldn't submit to social forces and powers outside of ourselves. The real issue is how do You do this in a communal setting and still maintain cordial relations with family, friends, and business associates? Life can sometimes feel like a big knot in the stomach, a lot of pressure which gives rise to this idea of dissatisfaction. It's why people say, "I need to get away," which is what *vacation* usually means. But You can't ever vacate Yourself or "get away" because wherever You go, *You* are there. What You want to do is be in a place that allows You to flow, to glow, to grow, to be *You*. You are truly wondrous, You're bountiful, beloved, and immortal! Part of being immortal is recognizing that Your eternal being is enhanced as the pressures decrease and as the true You emerges.

A Naomi story. After I was first paralyzed, I was in three different hospitals for a total of 144 days. We had just been brought to the 3rd hospital, after a total of thirty-six days in the first two. My assigned bed was in a shared room, smaller than the other places, and considerably darker. It was made more so by the fact that my side was not next to the window. The current occupant was quiet but liked to listen to the TV at a high volume. Funnily enough, I'm not a TV watcher; we don't have one in the house. My wonderful wife was a bit distraught, but so be it, and we had no idea of how long this would be. I was paralyzed. She was doing all the caring and worrying and taking care of the myriad household issues.

By the 3rd day, which was a Friday, she was so anxious for me that unbeknownst to me she went outside the room, burst into tears, and was found that way by the head nurse. The next thing I know, there are two people on my side of the room piling things on my bed (and me!), unplugging my special hospital bed[6], and moving the bed out of the room—to where, I had no idea. Nor did my wife.

Within minutes, though, I was "plugged in" and inflated in a private, well-lit, airy room on the other wing of the floor. The head nurse—Jessica was her name—couldn't bear to see my wife cry. She heard her story and told her, "Don't You worry. I'll take of everything."

And she did.

For the remainder of the over 100 days in that hospital, that was my room. Never shared. Big. Bright. Airy. Clean. No TV blaring.

My wife didn't rant. Didn't complain. She didn't need to do anything more than be herself: caring, loving. The result was extraordinary. In the words of the hospital's chief administrator: no one had ever had a private room for more than a week. And we were there for months!

Directing Yourself by Choosing Your GOALs

Here's a useful practice. In Your journal, write down the following: *Freedom without direction is chaos*[7]. Please write this phrase at the top of each page in Your journal for thirty consecutive days. Naomi was free from thinking about what others thought about her behavior, but she was structured by the values she herself had chosen and cherished. Now You'll be able to see this principle and think about it. You know what chaos is: it's destructive.

---

6   Long story but suffice it to say that it was an expensive, sophisticated air mattress specially designed for people who can't move. It's designed to help occupants avoid bedsores, a not uncommon painful and dangerous side effect of a long stay in bed.

7   With permission of my mentor and voice coach, Arthur Samuel Joseph.

Not just to Your psyche but to Your physical being. Chaos wreaks havoc with Your internal structure. It literally attacks Your physical being and sets up STRESS. And chronic STRESS can kill.

Chaos infiltrates Your heart, Your mind, and even Your bone structure. That's what chaos does. It doesn't build; it tears down. The *best* way to avoid that and to overcome it is to recognize that not only are You free to choose Your thoughts, but You will move inexorably, every single day, striving forward in the direction of Your goal/s. (GOAL stands for **G**o **O**ut and **A**chieve **L**ife.)

So now, I'd like You to say out loud what You wrote down: *Freedom without direction is chaos.* This is a vital tip because what Your lips articulate stimulates Your mind and Your heart. You can feel what a difference this makes. For Your benefit. For Your well-being. Please do this twice a day with feeling: once in the morning very soon after You wake up and once in the evening, close to when You're going to sleep. Saying the words becomes Your mantra, a slogan, and making it Yours enables You to internalize the thought: freedom without direction is chaos. And the corollary is: *I don't want to live with chaos; I prefer to live in harmony and I'm always striving forward.*

Generosity Sets You Free

We've talked about money. You do know the quote, "Money is the root of all evil." But this is not the correct quote! "The *lust* for money is the root of all evil,"[8] is the correct quote and the truth. Recall what my rich uncle taught: Money is an awful taskmaster but a highly beneficial and useful servant. If You let it, money can define Your status. With this wonderful strategy, You'll not allow money to define You or Your true worth.

Is this really possible? Yes. I know well several people who are enormously wealthy in terms of money and property. They are simultaneously generous, caring, empathetic people, who regularly work to be able to answer: how can I be of benefit?

Recall, the JOY of *living* can be summed up in a word: *giving*.

---

8   1 Timothy 6:10a.

Throughout the ages, there have been people whose names were synonymous with wealth. Today we have Bill Gates, Jeff Bezos, and Warren Buffet. Buffet has accumulated a vast fortune because from a very young age he realized that financial freedom with direction brings bounty and, in his case, great wealth. Those who followed his advice have gained fortunes, and those businesses that he has invested in have prospered, employing hundreds of thousands of people. Yet he still lives in the same modest home he has lived in for over fifty years. He recognizes that money is a process, it's a tool. It doesn't define him because he has nothing to prove.

A New Kind of FAST

Never look at anyone else. It's only about who You are. Who *are* You? Thinking about Yourself is not easy. It takes time. Effort. And determination. Each of which seem to be in short supply in our fast-paced, high-speed, always-on world. You can improve when You *decide* to use Your time to think about where You are in Your process. Time to determine Your values and remember to be Yourself.

And to remember that You don't need to prove Yourself.

Comparison is the death of true self-contentment.

—*John Powell, writer*

Oh yeah. "I know all this," You might say. But knowing and doing are two different and often competing issues. Determining to make the time to disconnect from such ubiquitous siren songs as social media, videos, gossip, online chat, et al., is a necessary first step in claiming Your ownership of the being called *You.*

Here's a highly effective, practical, and useful experiment. Set aside eight hours (!) one day per week to be free from the allure of "connectivity." Did I write, "eight hours"? Yes. And I urge You to make these eight *waking* hours. Example: try it from 8 a.m. until 4 p.m. one day per week. You are "fasting" from connectivity.

Impossible, You say. *Quite* possible! So, let's compromise and begin with four hours. With the goal of doing an eight-hour stretch within three months. After You have reached eight hours once per week, then You determine if You want to continue. I eagerly await Your communication.

Renunciation precedes regeneration.

This practice can move You away from being a slave to Your passions. Hopefully, You'll recognize the LIE of living as a slave to others. A LIE is a **L**ife-**I**nhibiting **E**xperience. Freeing Yourself from LIEs is the work of a lifetime.

Love Brings It All Together

Renunciation precedes regeneration. Once You become aware of the fact that we all participate in some activities where we seem to need the approval of others, You will begin to lessen and even abandon those practices. As You do so, You will regenerate and become more You.

Giving and gratitude are the two most human experiences bordering on the divine. Expressing these brings You joy wherein You don't need to prove Yourself. The direct result is a world of good, beneficial, bounty. You live and thrive in a world of abundance. As You realize Your special gifts, You will see that there is no other "You" and that You are complete.

Allow me to indulge You with one more Naomi story. I was to be released from hospital on January 13, 2005. Still paralyzed. We needed help around the clock. We found an agency and a capable person was referred. However, Naomi did not want any stranger, let alone a man, staying overnight in the house. Ah, but here's the rub. I couldn't turn over on my side by myself. In the hospital there was a "turning team" of two people, complete with back braces, who would turn me every four hours from one side to another to simulate a normal sleep position. What to do? My amazing wife, who stands 5'1" and weighs under 100 pounds, decided to literally take matters into her own hands.

You've probably heard of the story of someone pinned under a car and a mother or grandmother (!) lifting up the ton weight to rescue the victim, usually a child. May be apocryphal. Now I am 5'11" and by the time of

123

coming home, I weighed just 137 pounds. Just a bunch of protoplasm really. However, my amazing wife set her clock and every four hours, from 10 p.m. when our caretaker left, until 7 a.m. when he returned, Naomi would, by herself, manage to turn me from lying on my back to lying on one side and then, four hours later, to the other side. Every night. Night in. Night out. Week in, week out. For two years!

This, I submit, is love. *Love.*

No need to prove Yourself is perhaps the hardest level of joy to achieve. It takes time and effort. It will work miracles. And in a relatively short period of time.

Let Go. Let Love.

The Takeaways

The beauty of life emerges through struggle.

Later is the first step to never.

Comparison is the death of true self-contentment.

OWN it NOW.

Renunciation precedes regeneration.

Growth with Action

Write down three ways that show that You don't need to prove Yourself. Be creative.

_____

_____

_____

_____

In Your journal, write down three actions You will take in the next month, to Your benefit, which You will do to show that You don't need to prove Yourself.

_____

_____

_____

_____

You are determining Yourself by choice, not by chance. Journal about Your belief that You control Your time and Your scheduling of it here.

_____

_____

_____

_____

Strategy Eleven: How to Keep Smiling No Matter What

It was a cold, drizzly Monday morning in winter in a midsize New England town. Heather had on her hoodie. She was moving along towards a sixteen-story building, the tallest in the area, and one that had roof access (she'd found that out on Friday).

As she walked, looking down, she stepped on a card. It was blue. And she stopped just for a moment and looked at it a second time. It read, "KEEP SMILING." She picked it up and, with a wry expression, thought, *That's a sick joke.*

Just at that moment, someone passed on her left. "Good morning."

And then on her right. "Oh, good morning."

People were moving past her as she stood stock-still.

"Hello."

"Be well."

Heather had no idea what to do. This was to be her morning. This was it. The building would open in a few minutes. She knew how to access the roof. She was done—done with life.

"Stay dry."

Heather still didn't know what to do. She looked at the card again. *KEEP SMILING.* Oh, stop it. And she stood still. It seemed like ten minutes, though it was probably more like seconds. She crushed the card. Thrust it into her hoodie's pocket.

And turned around and walked away from her death.

That was six years ago. She still struggles, she tells me. But she's here.

A simple *KEEP SMILING* card.

And the greetings of people going about their normal days.

And it saved a life.

Smile It, Sing It, Say It

The strategy of this chapter, *keep smiling*, pulls together the threads running through all the rest. It continues to reveal the beautiful tapestry that is You.

"Keep smiling" assumes that You are already smiling. As we discussed in the "smile" strategy, the word SMILE is an acronym for **S**eeing **M**iracles **I**n **L**ife **E**veryday. In this chapter, we're going to discuss many other ways of determining and/or analyzing the *smile* concept from sources all over the world. Over time, people have given me insight into how they perceive aspects of everyday words that help us lay down positive tracks. This allows us to subtly replace other associations.

A simple example of this is "www." Ask anyone what "www" means and invariably they'll say it has something to do with the internet. But in our world—the world of the positive, purposeful, powerful, and pleasant— WWW stands for: Whata Wonderful World. Tip of the hat to wonderful Satchmo/Louis Armstrong for enabling the song of the same name to go viral and touch hundreds of millions, if not billions, of people worldwide. And whenever You hear even the opening bars of that song, You can't help but...smile.[9]

Music has such a way of influencing our emotions, doesn't it? We can use that power for good—we can use it to remind us to smile.

I have a good friend who's a leader in a swing band that plays a foot-stomping, dance-with-a-partner kind of jazz. He would begin training his band by having everyone play the notes just to get the feel of them.

---

9   Hear the song at: https://www.youtube.com/watch?v=CWzrABouyeE (over 40 million views!).

After a bit he'd say, "Okay...now that You know the notes, let's find the music." That's what we're doing with our 11 Strategies. We're finding the music in Your soul. Right now, let's enlarge the acronym SMILE to mean **S**ong **M**ovement **I**magination **L**aughter **E**nergy. Our little riff includes the word *laughter* and that is so fundamental to being human that You should do it daily (more on that later).

You've got to dance daily, even hourly, sing a joyful tune, and laugh out loud.

That's the feeling of, that's the meaning of, JOY.

Smiling is a reminder, singing is a reminder, and *speaking* is a reminder too. A phrase that I urge You to internalize and say is: "The world was created just for me." Does that sound egotistical? On the contrary, what that phrase means is that You have a responsibility and that Your thoughts and deeds make a difference. You are not a mood-controlled person but rather You control Your disposition. The world was created for You. Make a difference.

Calm and Aware

What's behind Your smiling face? A calm, aware mind. A serene mind.

The calmness of Your mind is a beautiful jewel of wisdom and is the result of a long and patient effort at self-control. Its presence indicates ripened experience and an understanding that You are a thought-evolved being. You increasingly and clearly see the internal relationships of things and actions as a result of cause and effect. You remain poised and serene. Calmness of mind is the hallmark of a well-lived, love-filled life.

With these 11 Strategies You are building practices to help You achieve this kind of mind. Calm and aware.

The Best Medicine

But being calm and aware does not keep You from exuberant laughter! Laughter bubbles up from serenity like fresh water from an underground spring.

A wondrous example of using this strategy of *laughter* is a man named Norman Cousins. In the 1960s, he contracted a very rare disease that was going to kill him within a matter of months. He consulted doctors on both coasts. Unfortunately, they all told him the same thing. He decided to take contrary action. He reasoned that if stress and genes activated this disease, then maybe his positive thinking and actions could reverse the process. He determined that laughter could be a cure for his situation.

Against every doctor's advice and doubt, he utilized every means possible to induce laughter and happiness into his life. After months of dedicated, focused activity, he got better. As he watched things that he knew were going to cause him to laugh, in time, the pain lessened. At times it even went away, and he became pain-free for longer and longer periods. He realized that the best medication was his meditation on laughter and its effect on his entire being.[10]

Because of his inspiration, I practice this regularly. Norman Cousins cured himself from a dreadful disease. He recognized that the mind is the master and that by using positive thinking he could think himself well. Was it a placebo? (Be aware: placebo is Latin for I shall be pleasing.) Was he just a special case? Read *Anatomy of An Illness*, his book about his journey, and You decide.

How Many Different Ways Can You SMILE?

The story of Norman Cousins tells us that we can go MAD—**M**ake **A** **D**ifference—by Sending My Inner Love Everywhere—another meaning for SMILE. Acronyms of SMILE can be found everywhere. Here are some acronyms that people from around the world have shared with me:

- Sound Moving Inexorably, Lovingly, Energetically

- Sending My Intentional Love Everywhere

- Streaming My Inner Love (to) Everyone

---

10 Here's some brief history in the form of a movie clip of Ed Asner playing Norman Cousins in a show which was based on Cousins's 1979 book, Anatomy of an Illness as Perceived by the Patient: Reflections on Healing and Regeneration: https://www.youtube.com/watch?v=t50r903AeHY.

- Spontaneous Magic In Loving Exuberantly

- Savoring Memories In Life Experiences

- Sending Music Inspiration Lovingly Everywhere

- Solving Mysteries In Life Everyday

- Scaling Mountains In Life Everyday

- Seeing Momentous Insightful Life Experiences

Find two positive ways of expressing it as an acronym for Yourself. I would love it if You sent them to me. If You do, I will try to use them, and if possible, give You credit. I would love to hear and see what You're doing with this tool. Smile, please. The world needs it and the world needs You.

The Magnificent FIGS

As we draw on this unique strategy, it's vital that You meet the inspiration for my life and the key person who enabled me to persevere and continue to always strive forward. Please meet Frances Ida Goldstein Shore—FIGS to her friends and family.

My mother.

Born in 1915 in Boston, Massachusetts, she was the second of four children. She was gregarious and generous from a very young age. And she also sported a port-wine stain birthmark over three-fourths of her face! Yet here's the wondrous part: not only was Frances undaunted, but according to family and close friends, she never even "noticed" that she had a "mark." Of course, she was taunted; kids can be cruel. Even adults. But this bountiful, beneficent being lived life to the full. She exhibited such a radiant smile and *joie de vivre* that almost everyone that came into her orbit was attracted to her.

Never the shrinking violet, she was outspoken and yet empathetic; after all, she knew about "issues" and struggles. She excelled at school and though she did not attend college, she did graduate near the top of her large high school class and secured a high paying job in the diamond industry—quite unusual for a young unmarried woman in those days.

She met and married my father, Bernard, who was a good-looking, well-dressed young man nicknamed "the duke" for his stylish apparel. He was shy and quiet compared to my mother, yet together they flourished. I was the oldest of three—I have two wonderful, successful sisters.

Throughout our growing-up years, we always knew and saw our mother's facial issues, yet they were "masked" not by makeup as much as by her beaming charisma.

Two quick stories might suffice.

The first happened when I was about fourteen. A friend was visiting our house. There were always kids visiting because my mother was a superb baker. Most people bought bakery goods, but my mother preferred baking apple pie, coffee cake, strudel, and more from scratch.

So, a friend was over. We're sitting at the kitchen table and savoring fresh-from-the-oven (cooled, but still hot) pie when my mother walks in. Without her usual pancake makeup. My friend dropped his fork and said, "Yikes! What happened to your mother!"

Well nothing. I looked and said so.

He said, pointing, "But look at her face!"

I looked. It was my mother, beaming. She didn't take offense. Just kept beaming and said, "Hi, Jeffrey. How's Your mother? How's Your sister? Did she really get accepted to Harvard?" Such nonchalance. Such composure. Such love.

Next short story: the supermarket near our house, Star Market by name, was putting in something called a Courtesy Booth. At another time it would've been named a "complaint department," but some clever person understood that accentuating the positive would be of benefit. Our family shopped there regularly, and the manager asked my mother if she would consider being the Courtesy Booth Person. She could set her own hours and just be herself in helping people and resolving any issues.

And so, Frances, aka FIGS, became the model for the Courtesy Booths throughout the twelve-store chain. She was the *face* of Star Market and made a difference (yes, she was MAD decades ago) for the customers, the store's bottom line, and the management. So much so that when she decided to retire some twelve years later, she was honored at a banquet with speeches, an award, a valuable Steuben glass vase, and a not inconsequential check. Apparently, the Courtesy Booth model of business increased the bottom line year over year for more than a decade by some 2.3%! In the grocery business, with its razor-thin margins, this was a major increase.

Third short story: sponge cake. As a teenager I drove a taxicab in my hometown of Brookline, Massachusetts. The company had several standing accounts. One was to pick up an eight-year-old boy in the morning, bring him to a school, and bring him back home in the early afternoon. Nice kid. Quiet. I tried to engage him in conversation and got few words in return. Until the third week. Throughout the ride to the school and on the way back, he kept saying "sponge cake." I asked him if he liked sponge cake. He just repeated, "Sponge cake."

Back home, I mentioned this sweet kid and his obsession with sponge cake to my mother. She said, "Okay, I'll make a sponge cake and You can bring it tomorrow." So, she did. I was actually looking forward to bringing the sponge cake.

As I walked the boy, Michael, to his house, I mentioned sponge cake. I knocked on the door and Michael's mother answered and hugged Michael. I then offered the sponge cake and said that my mother baked it specially for Michael because he had repeated "sponge cake" many times over the past two days.

Michael's mother began tearing up and said, "Please come in." We went into the kitchen. She told me "sponge cake" was Michael's dog and that the dog had died two days ago. *Yikes!* And Michael was a challenged kid with something called "autism." Bear in mind this is 1966. Very few people had such a diagnosis or knew what it was. My mother was heartbroken when she heard the story. As was I. But I was again moved by how loving and caring my mother was.

Coda: my younger sister has four daughters. One of them is autistic.

"Grammy" was a major force for good in their lives.

Frances is the source of my ability to overcome trauma. Difficulties. Negative thoughts. And I dare say she can be Your model as well.

Never Stop Giving

The famous phrase from Churchill uttered at a commencement address of American Combat pilots still resonates today:

Never Give Up! Never. Never. Never. NEVER!

Let's go to our CORE again (**C**ontinuous **O**ngoing **R**ejuvenating **E**nergy). Here's the essential aspect of "keep smiling." In one word: giving. You know intellectually, emotionally, and fervently that giving is what You want to do in life. As an acronym, GIVE means **G**rowing **I**ncreasing **V**ibrant **E**nergy. Miracles will happen for You and others when You are harmonized with the LAW of attraction. LAW stands for **L**ove **A**nd **W**isdom. If You're focusing and using VVE (**V**erbalizing, **V**isualizing, **E**motionalizing) with the goal of helping people, everything is possible. Think again about Norman Cousins. Think what You can do for those who don't have potable water and other essentials—think about what You can do by using Your positive, powerful, purposeful, pleasant energy.

Even though we all have an expiration date, as You keep smiling, You will keep sowing, harvesting, giving, and receiving. Keep on because You are eternal.

Smiling is one of the most effective therapeutic mechanisms for generating positive emotions. It has been observed that babies smile as much as 400 times per day. Adults, maybe twenty. You don't have to be a child to smile more. Be a conscious adult and double the number to forty and You'll be in the top 1% of purposeful, powerful, pleasant people in the world.

Here's a simple effective plan that everyone can do: Give KEEP SMILING cards. Physically or by email. Make an agreement with Yourself to give cards at least twice a week. This will build Your giving muscle. Order cards. They're free. Just pay postage. Or go on the website www.thedailysmile. com and you can send five cards at one time electronically. Totally free. Do this twice per week and You touch ten people. Continue this every month and You'll touch positively 500+ people per year. And encourage everyone You know to do the same. It's easy, free, and funn.

Do this weekly and don't skip. Then plan to increase Your level of giving. Maybe fifteen per week and then twenty. To put this into perspective, there are some devoted distributors that have standing orders for 750 cards every sixty days. Everybody is here to grow at their own pace. Create Your own program. (CREATE means **C**ausing **R**ethinking **E**nabling **A**ll **T**o **E**xcel.) Be the model You want to emulate.

Thinking is wonderful, speaking is better.

Action is the best.

The Takeaways

One Keep Smiling card saved a life.

WWW = Whata Wonderful World

Shift Happens.....too many people drop the f.

Internalize: the world was created just for me.

A calm aware mind is a jewel.

Find the music.

FIGS was undaunted and radiated success. No matter the circumstance.

Growth with Action

Create three acronyms for SMILE. Have fun !

_____

_____

_____

Commit to distributing some number of Keep Smiling cards every month.

_____

_____

_____

How did You feel when You read Heather's story? Please read it again. Write down Your thoughts.

_____

_____

_____

How do You feel when You read about FIGS? Write down Your thoughts.

_____

_____

_____

Write three action items that You will take in the next thirty days to activate Your giving muscle. Which one will You resolve to continue for 183 days?

_____

_____

_____

PART 3

Afterword: Taking Joy to the Next Level

"You better call his parents. We're not sure if he'll make it another day."

This was the evening of June 22, 1972. I was in a hospital in Westchester County, NY. Unconscious. Just rescued from a collision on the freeway. A driver fell asleep at the wheel and his full-size Buick hurtled over the median and hit my VW Beetle. Head-on. No seat belts. I was twenty-four.

The doctors were telling my friend, Colleen, the head of production for our high fashion boutique company, to call my loved ones. She had been following my car when the collision happened. Colleen called my girlfriend, who called my parents. They came.

As You know, I did survive. Broken right femur—broken in several places. Glass on my body and face. Thankfully, some top surgeons pieced together my femur (thighbone) with two state-of-the-art titanium plates, each twelve inches long and held in place with ten two-inch-long unique metal screws. Over the course of six months, with intense prayer, therapy, and love, I was able to exert pressure on the leg and learned to walk again. Being twenty-four helped. Over the course of the next two years, I had two more operations: one each to remove a plate and ten screws. The bone had healed. As had I...physically, mentally, and spiritually.

Yes, I was reborn.

Why do I relate this story? To ask You the question I asked myself then: Where do You go from here?

There's a lot of good useful *information* in this book.

The goal, however, is *transformation.*

You are an alchemist. In centuries past, alchemy was the process of trying to transmute base metal into precious metal. It couldn't (and can't) be done. However, the cognoscenti knew that the true transmutation was of the physical and ephemeral into the soul-ful and eternal. This can be done. This is our journey with the JOY of *living.* You are precious. The key is to recognize this and ever strive forward to live life to the full. Once You grasp this, and internalize, utilize, and leverage these Strategies, You will be a **transformer.** You will become not just blessed; You will *be* a blessing.

This is the highest calling in the world.

It took me decades to discover these Strategies, but it was worth every moment of struggle, because You just read this book. You are a **transformer**, now Go Make a Difference.

Pass along these Strategies to others, share this book with them, and transmit Your Joy to them, and they will transmit it to others and together we will be the change that the world needs right now . . .

Most Sincere Best Wishes for Continuing Success in All Endeavors,

barry

PS: SMILE as YOU see, internalize, and utilize WWW

About the Author

Barry's Mission is to transform the world through JOY.

He is called The Ambassador of Joy. Barry is a Motivational Speaker as well as a Serial Entrepreneur with two multi-million dollar exits and 3 issued patents.

He founded The JOY of LIVING Institute ™ to enable people everywhere in the World to find the JOY in LIVING. To this end he also hosts the popular podcast The JOY of LIVING which has over two million downloads in its first 19 months.

Barry is the man who was completely paralyzed overnight from a rare disease. He emerged through years of physical therapy from being a quadriplegic to now swimming 2 miles/day, 6 days/week.

Throughout the years of recovery, he envisioned and articulated Systems that are now embodied in the "11 Strategies" which enable people of all ages and backgrounds to Live in JOY, daily. No matter the circumstances.

His journey to regain mobility pushed him to Go MAD: Make A Difference. He welcomes YOU to go MAD.

Barry's Keep Smiling Movement has distributed over TWO million Keep Smiling Cards, in 27 languages, throughout the world for free.

This book, The JOY of LIVING, is his paean to humanity and his legacy.

Acknowledgments

The most important ship You ever sail is that called relationship.

People are the raison d'etre of living in service.

I humbly and fully acknowledge the remarkable people in my life who have consciously or otherwise influenced me for the better.

Certainly, my family takes center stage: my parents, Bernard and Frances (aka FIGS) were central. So too my dear beloved sisters, Laraine and Barbara; and their extended and growing families.

Imagine being at the dinner table (or riding in the car or sitting on the porch) singing joyous songs together!? That was our youth. Was it always so. No. We're human; and it is their very humanity that makes this journey possible.

And to our son Ezra. His stellar wife, Shoshi. Their/our (currently) two sons: MNE and BZO.

Thank You my dear family.

Friendships; a number of them spanning 6 or 7 decades were/are cornerstones. More recent ones have helped complete this book with their keen insights and loving care.

To You, wonder filled people: past, current, and future friends, my deepest Appreciation for Your concern, advice (whether solicited or not), and demonstration of the core value of Friend.

Teachers have played a significant role in shaping, molding, guiding my thoughts, words, and deeds. In the latter two, the errors must be admitted as entirely my own. If there is a positive impact that I have made, then credit most certainly accrues to my teachers. There are no words to describe the kindness, attentiveness, and honesty which I witnessed and absorbed. Your words and most telling, Your actions, made a difference. May You continue to inspire, grow, and flourish.

To the Creator. Imagine addressing GOD.

YOUR presence in my life is manifest. Certainly, everyone now knows about my paralysis. My emergence, almost as the chrysalis into the butterfly, as a husband of 44 years (yes, my Naomi gets mention in the same paragraph as GOD!), a father of 32 years, a grandfather of 3.5 years, as a student of 72 years with a Sense of Wonder (the SOW factor) of an 8 year-old. Childlike, not childish. All and every accomplishment of Benefit in Service is to YOU.

With deep humility and JOY filled SONG i raise my arms in THANKS and PRAISE. May i prove myself worthy of YOUR infusing me with LIFE.

Joy Vocabulary

The Purpose here is to Unlock the Power and Secrets of Everyday Words and Terms. You are encouraged to visit the Joy Vocabulary and submit Your very own Positive, Powerful and Purposeful acronym/s as we continue to grow this database of JOY. We will endeavor to acknowledge two new entries with each weekly publication of the Touch of Barry Newsletter.

ABLE: Always Believe Love Exists	**HAS**: Heart And Soul
ACT: Always Courageous Thinking	**IS**: Inspire Smiles
ALL: Always Love Life	**JAW**: Joy At Work
ASAP: Always Say A Prayer	**KIND**: Keep Inspiring Noble Deeds
ASK: Always Seek Kindness	**LIFE**: Living Inspirationally For Eternity
BABE: Be A Blessing Everyday	**LOG**: Love Of Giving
BIG: Believe In Giving	**MAN**: Manifesting Amazing Nobility
BOSS: Being Of Service Successfully	**NUT**: Never Underestimate Thanking
BOWL: Becoming One With Life	**POOP**: Power Of One Person
DO: Divine Order	**POT**: Power of Thought
DOG: Doing Of GOOD	**RICH**: Rejoicing In Choosing Happiness
EGO: Edging God Out	**SOUL**: Song Of Unlimited LIFE
GOAL: Go Out & Achieve Life	**UP**: Unlimited Potential
GOT: Gift Of Time	**WOW**: Words Of Wisdom

Visit **www.barryshore.com/words** to browse the Joy Vocabulary and submit Your very own acronym/s.

Testimonials

Delightfully fun and a master of alliteration, Barry Shore blissfully fuses the wisdom of experience with the wonder of youth. Those in need of uplift count on this Ambassador of Joy to entertain them with his wit and challenge their mindsets with a ready supply of creative acronyms. As pleasant behind the scenes as he is endearing in front of a mic, Barry Shore is a man I'm very happy to call my friend!

Maura Sweeney - Ambassador of Happiness ®, Podcaster and International Speaker

I love working with entrepreneurs who understand that life is about more than making money, it's also about helping people and having fun in the process, and that's something that Barry Shore certainly knows about. Not only will the tips and strategies he shares in The Joy of Living help you to overcome the obstacles you're facing, but they will help you to find passion and purpose in your daily life...and to live a life of joy.

David Meltzer, Co-founder of Sports 1 Marketing, former CEO of Leigh Steinberg Sports & Entertainment agency, best-selling author, podcaster, business coach and philanthropist

Each week I'm privileged to interview the world's most inspirational and successful people on my show. Few have the energy, genuineness, and soul of Barry Shore. This book is an extension of his incredible story and a blueprint for truly living your life each and every day with JOY and fulfillment. The science is quite clear, happier people are healthier people. I simply cannot recommend this book highly enough. It is what the world truly needs right now!

Dr. Richard Shuster – Internationally renowned Influencer, Host of the Daily Helping Podcast, Media Expert, and TEDx Speaker.

Mr. Barry Shore - Our Symbol, Resonant Figure & Champion for Global Joy. Having been around the transformational expert/guru block quite a bit, I saw immediately in Barry how consistently and unabashedly he showed what joy can look like in its truest and more genuine form.

He enabled me to look deep into my own soul - to find that honest place where resignation and cynicism meet possibility and had me decide fully which side I was going to be on. Barry is the greatest champion and stalwart steward for Joy in this precious Globe of ours.

I am deeply honored to be his friend and his fan and invite all of you to be the same.

Sunil Bhaskaran, Founder of Global Business Communities.

When I founded BNI in 1985 it was based on the principle of GIVING. Today, with over 275,000 members worldwide, BNI is the world's largest business networking group. Barry Shore's The JOY of LIVING is summed up in one word: GIVING. My hope is that he touches 100 times as many people with his important and vital message. You will be healthier AND wealthier for using this guide.

Dr. Ivan Misner, NY Times Bestselling Author and Founder of BNI

I've helped many authors become bestselling authors. Barry Shore is one of the most consistently joy-filled people I've ever met. He's an amazing man with an amazing story. Read his book now.

Steve Harrison, co-founder, www.NationalPublcitySummit.com

Barry Shore is a living miracle. By all accounts, he should be pushing up daisies. His remarkable journey from death's doorstep to becoming a beacon of joy inspired me to co-author the #1 bestseller, The Magic of Everyday Giving with him. Barry is one of the most influential people of our time.

Dick Larkin, best selling author

As an International Publicist and as Executive Director of The Keep Smiling Movement, I can say with full confidence that the Ambassador of Joy brings it full circle! You will Keep Smiling way past the end!

Dr. Andrea Adams-Miller, CNLP, CHt, BCBP. CLL, CEO, The Keep Smiling Movement

Barry Shore is a living legend. He is beloved by so many people for his wit, his wisdom and his love of life. His story of overcoming paralysis and always finding the good in things is inspirational. The ambassador of joy will make you smile, make you think and change your life for the better.

Mike Duffy Founder The Happiness Hall Of Fame, TEDx Berkeley talk

Imagine sitting next to an irrepressible, exuberant, septuagenarian elbow to elbow who you never met before...for 3 solid days. Yes, I drank a few glasses of wine as we both imbibed the mind-expanding wisdom at the Wizard Academy. More importantly, this being has become a good friend and I am proud to recommend this book and the powerful, purposeful, positive work that he is doing. Use it. You'll be better off mentally and physically.

Larry Bradley, World Renowned CEO, Speaker, and Author

Barry Shore has shown in his widely-acclaimed podcasts that he can make a happy acronym out of any word, and in this book you'll find them along with wisdom and humor toward coping with life's hurdles. Let me suggest an apt acronym for The Joy of Living: READ, which stands for "Rousing, Entertaining And Delightful!"

Diane Medved, Ph.D. psychologist, columnist and author of 7 books, most recently Don't Divorce: Powerful Arguments for Saving and Revitalizing Your Marriage.

The JOY of LIVING. Read it. Use the tips and tools. Take Action. This is Your handbook for Success in life.

Dr. Greg S. Reid, Award-Winning Author, Keynote Speaker and Film Producer

Almost 40 years ago I broke new ground in the healing process with Love, Medicine and Miracles. As the decades have shown there IS a correlation between Your Mind/Heart and Living Healthfully. Today the message of JOY in this book The JOY of LIVING by a living example is needed for our beleaguered pandemic world. Pick up a Copy. Even better: USE the material here and Transform Your Life and those You LOVE. I'm giving You this RX. Barry is a success in the experience of life. Take it from me and learn from him. Read his book and gain his wisdom.

Bernie Siegel, MD author of No Endings Only Beginnings and Love Medicine & Miracles

I celebrate You, dear Barry. You are clearly an inspiration and an example of what it takes to truly live integrally...doing and being Your best. God Bless.

Arthur Samuel Joseph, Founder Vocal Awareness Institute, voted Best of the Best by YPO

WOW! Being within the voice of Barry Shore, the Ambassador of Joy is Happiness. Period.

Edwin Edebiri, MBA, Chief Happiness Officer

Barry Shore. What a great man! What a great program! Probably the best program ever, zoom or otherwise! Thank you for having him speak to us. Too bad meeting in-person is going to be delayed again, but these Zoom meetings are working out well. Keep up the good work.

Gary Mukai, Rotarian for 45 Years

Got your new book. Wow! It is YOU. If I can beam you into a book, this would be it. Thanks, and I hope your message of JOY resonates with every reader.

H. Hasenfeld, World Famous Diamantaire

Recommended Reading

Some great books/essays with insightful learning potential

Over the years I have been on a physical and spiritual journey and have read dozens of wonderful books/essays. I would like to share my recommendations of some of my favorites.

Yes, I recommend all of these to You as possible resources regardless of where you are on life's path.

Consider making it Your personal Goal to read one great book/essay every month that can inspire Your life for the better in some way.

BONUS: almost all are short. And Long on Impact.

Visit **www.barryshore.com/reading** for the complete list.

Should You decide to read any of the above – I hope You find the Peace, Contentment, Happiness and Success You are searching for as You travel life's highways.

> *"Five years from today you will be the same as you are today except for the books you read and the people you meet."*
>
> Charlie "Tremendous" Jones